DREAMS

DREAMS

DREAMS

a teenager's guide to dream interpretation

LORI REID

Cover illustration by
David Scutt

SCHOLASTIC

For Sophie and Alasdair
with my love

Scholastic Children's Books,
Commonwealth House, 1-19 New Oxford Street
London WC1A 1NU, UK
a division of Scholastic Ltd
London ~ New York ~ Toronto ~ Sydney ~ Auckland

First published in the UK by Scholastic Ltd, 1997

ISBN 0 590 19568 9

Typeset by TW Typesetting, Midsomer Norton, Avon
Printed by Cox and Wyman Ltd, Reading, Berks.

10 9 8 7 6 5 4 3 2 1

ACKNOWLEDGEMENTS

I really could not have accomplished the work on this book without the help, encouragement, support and advice from my daughter, Sophie. So thank you, and a big hug, for being there for me, Sophie.

A very special thank you, too, to Kirstie Russell, not only for all the vivid dreams she sent me but also for the enthusiasm she has shown for this book. I am indebted to both Dr F J MacFarlane Reid AFBPsS, CPsychol and to Mrs P Champness, Chartered Clinical Psychologist with the NHS for generously giving me so much of their time and advice. And I can't thank enough all the terrific young people who have talked endlessly to me or who have let me learn from their dreams. My gratitude in particular to: Marie, Rachel, Emma, Vicky, Alex, Jenny, Ben, Ali, Tom, Hari, Sarah, Hannah, Kerry and Nicki. May all your dreams be happy ones.

Contents

Chapter 1

Dreams

Why dream?

Dreams

Moving pictures

How often do you write notes to remind yourself of things you have to do? Like, 'Don't forget to take games kit to school tomorrow', or, 'Remember to post Aunt Mabel's birthday card', or even, 'Must buy that new CD on Saturday'.

Or perhaps you keep a diary. Lots of people do. Some even manage to write their diaries for most of their lives, finding a few quiet minutes in the evening to jot down their thoughts and record what's been happening to them in the day.

Well, whether you're the sort of person who has to scribble reminders on yellow sticky bits of paper, or whether you make regular entries into your diary, what you are in fact doing is writing messages to yourself. It's as if one part of you is communicating with another part.

And that's just what dreaming is like – it's you sending messages to yourself in your sleep. When you dream, what's happening is that your unconscious mind is talking to your conscious mind. It's all the same mind, just different departments.

Your dream, then, is the message that you're sending between those departments. Like a diary entry, it may consist of memories and impressions of the day, things that people said to you, information that you learned, observations that you made, events that took place. Or, like a reminder, your dream could be a note from yourself to yourself containing advice, comments or encouragement about the way your life is going.

But even though you're talking to yourself, your dreams are presented in a different language – one that sometimes you didn't even know you knew. This language is mainly visual and it uses images which need to be interpreted in order to understand properly the message they contain. That's just what this book is setting out to do. It's giving you the opportunity to translate your dream in the same way as you might use a French/English dictionary to translate a piece of written French.

Except the language in this A-Z is Image/English!

Whatever the message, your dreams will always be fascinating and visually exciting. Dreams are your own built-in movies, virtual reality without the cumbersome helmet. And like movies, dreams come in different types: some are thrilling, some are scary, some are virtual horror stories, some are romantic, some are even erotic. All are mini motion pictures, adventures that are packed with kaleidoscopic colour, full of characters and scenery, actions and feelings.

But the best bit of all, in most of your dreams, is that *you* get to be the star!

Why are dreams important?

Our dreams are important because they:

▶ replay and sort through the things that happen to us in the day and somehow make sense of our thoughts and feelings before they are stored away.

▶ act as safety valves, helping us to release the upsets, the tension and frustration we felt in the day.

▶ bring our problems and our fears to our attention so that we can understand them and try to resolve them when we wake up.

▶ give us messages from deep inside our unconscious minds, sometimes in the form of advice, guidance, reminders or even warnings about future events.

▶ can show us how to make the right decisions and prepare us for what will happen when we are awake.

▶ provide fun, fantasy and light relief. In dreams we can become anyone we want, do anything we like and even snog anyone we fancy.

If we're not given the chance to sleep and dream we may:

▶ compensate by day-dreaming instead.

▶ become irritable.

▶ find it difficult to concentrate during the day.

▶ grow forgetful and lose our power of memory.

▶ become mentally and physically ill.

Ten most commomn dream themes

By asking thousands of people what they dream about, researchers have found that some topics come up much more frequently than others. They call these *common dream themes*. They include:

1. **Flying:** Either the dreamer is actually flying through the air or he/she dreams about a bird or an aeroplane flying in the sky. Dreams about flying reveal something about the dreamer's ambitions in life.

2. **Climbing:** Like flying, this dream is also concerned

13

with ambition, climbing up the ladder, trying to get to the top, that sort of thing.

3. **Falling:** The opposite of flying and climbing, dreams about falling have something to do with a fear of failure.

4. **Fleeing:** This is one of the most common of the themes that people of all ages tend to have. It includes dreams about both running away and about being chased, so these can often turn into nightmares. This type of dream reflects the fears and anxieties that happen to us or that we feel and think about in our waking lives.

5. **Travel:** Whether on foot or in a vehicle (which can include things like bikes, rollerblades, skateboards, skis, etc), dreams about travel or movement show us the sort of progress we are making in our lives or they say something about how we are getting on at the present time.

6. **Water:** In our dreams water represents our feelings and emotions.

7. **Sex:** People start to dream about sex from around puberty and from then onwards it becomes one of the most frequent themes that we dream about. These are also known as erotic dreams. In Victorian times dreaming about sex was considered unhealthy and was severely discouraged. Nowadays, however, we regard having erotic dreams as a perfectly natural part of human experience.

8. Embarrassment: This category includes finding yourself in a public place either inappropriately dressed, in the nude or even sitting on the toilet. In fact, any sort of scene where you feel out of place or which makes you squirm. These embarrassment dreams, where people are watching or laughing at you, reveal a fear of making a fool of yourself in your waking life.

9. Death: No way near as sinister as they sound, dreams about death and dying usually foretell that big changes are about to take place in your life.

10. Being late: These dreams include missing trains or arriving too late to sit an exam. They're connected with achievement, with wanting to win or to be a success in life, but secretly fearing that we can't quite make the grade. These dreams show that we're afraid of failure and that we're worried about disappointing ourselves and those we love.

Six types of dreams

As well as discovering common themes that come up time and again in our dreams, researchers have also found that dreams can be categorized into different *types*. For example, some dreams appear just to record the events of the day whilst others can give us glimpses of events that are likely to happen in the future. And others still will solve our problems and unravel mysteries that have been puzzling us in our waking lives. This shows that even whilst we are asleep, our minds are able to process information on several different levels, sifting through the things that have happened to us in the day, and picking out just the right sort of message to send back that will be useful to us when we wake up.

Here are the six most common types of dreams that people tend to have.

Factual dreams

We tend to think that dreams are all loaded with messages which we need to interpret and work out and, on the whole, many of them are indeed like that. But we must also recognize that a lot of our dreams are what's known as factual dreams and these are not necessarily laden with meaning.

Factual dreams simply record, finish off or replay some event that took place that day in the dreamer's waking life, rather like holding up a photograph of a scene before sticking it into the great 'photograph album' of that person's memory bank.

Another type of factual dream that can occur is really quite intriguing. Here, the dream weaves into a story a sound or a smell that the dreamer picks up while he or she is still fast asleep. For example, a ringing doorbell might be woven into a dream of a wedding scene with ringing church bells. Or the smell of frying bacon may be threaded into a dream about a lavish banquet in which the dreamer is the guest of honour. Factual dreams are sometimes also known as 'residual' dreams, whereas those that weave in sounds and smells are called 'vigilant' dreams.

A typical factual dream...
Even if you were to remember this sort of dream, it

probably wouldn't leave you with very vivid images, and it wouldn't necessarily stir up your feelings to any great degree. We have a lot more dreams every night than we actually remember when we wake up and many of these will be of the 'residual' type, those that basically tidy up the things that took place in the day. The 'vigilant' type of dream, on the other hand, is a little different and probably makes you smile when you realize what triggered it off – like a car back-firing in the road outside, for example, or your neighbour's dog barking at the milkman. 'Vigilant' dreams are a proof that although we may be asleep, our brains are still active and alert (vigilant) to what's going on in the environment around us.

Prophetic dreams

Prophetic dreams are warning dreams. They show us events that will happen in the future. For example, you might dream about a plane crash and when you wake up next morning you hear in the news that a jumbo jet plummeted into the Atlantic Ocean and a massive rescue mission is under way to find the survivors. Or else, you might dream about a friend you haven't seen for a couple of years and, would you believe it, he rings you up the very next day and says he'd like to come and visit you at the weekend. People have been having prophetic dreams since the year dot and in fact the Bible is full of these stories. Take, for example, the one about Joseph – the chap with the 'Amazing Technicolor Dream Coat'.

In that story the Pharaoh had a dream about seven fat cows followed by seven lean ones which Joseph interpreted quite correctly as a warning that a severe famine would follow after seven years of plenty. By taking note of this dream and stock-piling food to tide them over the bad

17

years, Joseph and the Pharaoh saved the Egyptian people from starvation.

Many other prophetic dreams have been recounted throughout history, usually preceding a major disaster of some sort like the eruption of a volcano or the sinking of the *Titanic*. In fact, the author Graham Greene, wrote that he had foreseen in a dream the disaster that occurred to the *Titanic* a few nights before it sank. Abraham Lincoln, too, dreamed about his own death. He heard the mourners crying and saw his own body lying in state just a few days before he was assassinated by John Wilkes Booth. Other precognitive dreams include people who dream about the names of the winners in horse races.

Many laboratory experiments have taken place into precognitive dreams and countries like the USA and Russia have invested lots of money into this kind of paranormal research. Although it's difficult to prove conclusively, it has been recognized that some people do have prophetic dreams in their lives even though they may choose to put the events down to coincidence.

A typical prophetic dream...
If you're used to having this sort of dream, you'll usually know as soon as you wake up that your dream has given you advance information about something that is going to happen. People who have prophetic dreams have a kind of sixth sense and have probably been having prophetic dreams since they were children. In fact, young people tend to be more sensitive to this type of dream than adults. But many people have this sort of dream, although they tend not to remember it, or take no notice of it until the event they dreamt about actually takes place in real life. Then the dream immediately comes flooding back to them and it can leave them feeling quite stunned.

Problem-solving dreams

If you ever have a problem that you need to work out, whether it's an emotional worry, a decision you have to make, or a piece of homework you simply can't understand, you should think about it just before you fall asleep and quietly ask your subconscious to show you how to solve it in your dream that night. If you're lucky you'll have what's known as a 'problem-solving dream' and when you wake up in the morning you'll have the answer you need. Try it. With a bit of practice it can really achieve some startling results. Several inventors throughout history have admitted that some of their best inventions came to them in a dream like this.

For example, a dream about Indian natives stabbing the air with spears that had eye-holes in their tips gave Elias Howe the inspiration to pioneer the sewing machine. A dream about a snake with its tail in its mouth revealed the structure of the benzene molecule to the German chemist, Friedrich Kekulé. And those of you who are completely puzzled by quantum mechanics can blame it all on a dream which first gave the idea to Niels Bohr, the famous Nobel prize-winning physicist!

A typical problem-solving dream...
This may have you leaping out of bed crying 'Eureka!' Others may find the answer will come to them the next day.

Recurring dreams

Some people have exactly the same dream over and over again for months and, sometimes, even for years. These are known as recurring dreams and it's believed that they happen again and again because the dreamer simply isn't taking notice of the message that is being delivered by the dream. It's a bit like a friend who's trying to attract your attention from the other end of the street by waving and calling your name. She'll go on waving her hand in the air and shouting louder and louder until you finally notice her. It's only when you finally get the message that she'll stop waving and calling out to you. And that's just what it's like with recurring dreams. They will go on happening until the dreamer recognizes the message and deals with it. Once that happens, the recurring dreams stop.

A typical recurring dream...
repeats itself again and again, sometimes over successive days or weeks or, if the problems in waking life are not sorted out, it can go on recurring over many years.

Nightmares

Nightmares are terrifying. Vivid and frightening, they may contain several dream themes like being chased or running away, falling or drowning, or monsters and dangerous life-threatening situations. Dream researchers have found that children and young people tend to have more nightmares than adults do. Sometimes, people have these frightening dreams after watching a horror movie that's upset them, or when they're feverish and not feeling very well or because they go to bed on a full stomach. In general, though, nightmares are brought on by fears and anxieties in our waking lives. For instance, they might occur when we are under pressure, such as during exams, or when we are confronted with a serious problem that we don't know how to handle, or when we're scared of someone or something. If these same fears go on happening to us, then we may get the same nightmare again and again. Like the recurring dreams, it's only when we find a way to resolve our problems that these frightening dreams will stop.

A typical nightmare...
is unmistakable because it startles us awake, panting for breath, pouring with perspiration and with our heart pounding in our chest. Relief is sweet when we wake up and realize it was just a bad dream but, all the same, it still takes time to calm down and get over it.

Lucid dreams

A lucid dream is fairly rare and is more likely to occur early in the morning just as we come out of deep sleep or else when we take a cat-nap. It's been described as a dream within a dream because although we are dreaming, we know that we're dreaming and we can actually make things happen or direct what goes on in our dream, just like a director controls the actions or the actors in a film. Spooky or what?

Actually, a lot of serious research is taking place into lucid dreams because scientists believe they can be very useful, especially when we have problems to solve because we can get the dream to sort it all out and find a solution for us without our even having to lift a finger.

A typical lucid dream...
is one where you don't feel as if you've fallen asleep yet because everything seems so real and you think that you're still awake but – you *know* that you are dreaming. One of the big tell-tale clues here is that you recognize things that are wrong or absurd. For instance, in an ordinary dream if you were flying you would take it for granted that you *could* fly. In a lucid dream, however, you would 'know' it

was impossible to fly, so you would *say to yourself*, 'Hey, hang on a minute, it isn't possible to fly so I must be dreaming'. Or else you might dream that you go to sit in your favourite chair and find that the legs have been sawn off. If it's an ordinary dream, you would accept that the legs were missing but if it's a lucid dream, you would twig that that's not right at all. At other times, you can even see yourself lying there fast asleep inside your own dream! It really is quite a strange experience and you usually wake up with a terrific sense of achievement as if you had just climbed up to the top of Everest.

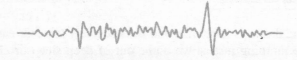

The pioneers in dream analysis

Throughout history, people have been fascinated by their dreams. Some really early writings dating right back to as long ago as 5000 BC contain explanations and meanings of dreams that were recounted by the Babylonians, Assyrians and Mesopotamians. In those days it was generally thought that dreams were messages sent by the gods – good dreams came from the good spirits and the bad ones from evil demons.

It's interesting that even in those times people dreamt about flying, although according to their interpretation this dream image meant certain death.

The Bible, of course, is full of stories about dreams, many containing prophecies and predictions of things to come. However, all civilizations right across the world have rich traditions in dreams and dream-lore. The Australian Aborigines, for example, believe in the

Dreamtime which created heaven, earth and all people. The Indians, writing in 1500 BC, believed that a dreamer's character had to be taken into account when interpreting his or her dream, which is very much what we also believe today. And as long ago as 500 BC, the Chinese recognized that dreams fit into different categories, and wrote about the differences between factual dreams, happy dreams, sad dreams and nightmares.

Perhaps the biggest name of early times in dream interpretation was Artemidorus who was born in Ephesus, in Asia Minor, and who lived in the second century AD. He wrote a very learned book which, in some ways, treated the interpretation of dreams a bit as we do today. The most important advance he made was to teach people that the same image in dreams could mean different things to different people. For instance, the colour white for one person could represent a wedding gown, whilst for another it might symbolize the lilies growing in his or her mum's front garden.

However, despite all the work on dream interpretation that came after Artemidorus, not much real progress was made in understanding dreams until the 19th century and the arrival of psychoanalysis. Since that time, a great deal of scientific research into both sleep and dreaming has taken place. Thanks to modern research, we now know a lot more about the mechanisms involved in sleeping and dreaming and, by collecting and analysing thousands of dreams, analysts have been able to discover the meanings behind the symbols and images that we dream about every night.

But none of these insights could have been made without the work of the early pioneers who set the ball rolling in the field of scientific dream research. Of these, four names in particular stand out: Freud, Jung, Adler and Perls.

Sigmund Freud (1856–1939)

Born in Austria, Freud is perhaps the best-known psychiatrist who ever lived. He was the founder of psychoanalysis and pioneered the study of the unconscious mind. Freud's interest in dream analysis grew from his work with people who were mentally disturbed. He believed that the answers to his patients' problems could be found by understanding and working out their dreams. He lived at a time when many people repressed their feelings, especially their sexual urges, so he came to believe that it was through dreams that people expressed their sexual anxieties, their fantasies and their needs. Interestingly, Freud and his theories keep going in and out of fashion, and, although we now realize there's a lot more to dreams than just sex, we still owe a great debt to Sigmund Freud for showing us the important link between our dreams and our subconscious personalities.

Carl Gustav Jung (1875–1961)

Another, equally famous, early pioneer in the field of psychiatry was Carl Jung (pronounced *yung*) who was born in Switzerland. Jung studied and worked with Freud, but he had broader vision and later disagreed with him principally over the importance that Freud gave to suppressed sexual desires as the cause of psychological problems. Jung widened and advanced the work on dream interpretation, devoting a great deal of attention to dream images and symbols which he called archetypes. He believed in the theory that people dream on two levels. He suggested, firstly, that we each draw from our own experiences and associations but that, secondly, we are also able to tap into a universal reservoir of memories and experiences which are common to everyone. This he called 'the collective unconscious', which is a bit like the World Wide Web which everyone can tap into whenever they want to find something out. Jung quite rightly believed that dreams have a much wider function than simply expressing our sexual desires. He recognized that we can all learn about ourselves through our dreams and that we can use the messages we receive from our subconscious to help us in our lives.

Alfred Adler (1870–1937)

Adler was also born in Austria and lived and worked at the same time as Freud and Jung. He became interested in the aspect of human behaviour that concerned personal power – how powerful or ineffectual a person felt in his or her environment or how much personal influence an individual could wield in his/her immediate circle. It was Adler who first discussed the concepts of inferiority and superiority conflicts and also of sibling rivalry. If you have brothers or sisters you probably know exactly what that means and what it feels like, because it's the term given to the jealousy or the competition that can arise between brothers and sisters. When it came to working with dreams, Adler tended to think that it is only through our dreams that we can compensate for our inadequacies. He believed that dreams are a form of wish-fulfilment. For example, if someone had a damaged leg he/she would dream of walking, running and jumping just like everyone else in order to make up for his/her disability in waking life. For Adler, then, dreaming was a convenient way of righting the balance for Nature's mistakes.

Fritz Perls (1893–1970)

Unlike the other three giants in psychoanalysis, Fritz Perls was born in America. He is most famous for inventing a particular type of psychotherapy known as Gestalt. He used dream therapy in treating his patients and strongly believed that symbols in dreams are personal to the dreamer. He taught his patients to 'role play' their dreams, that is, to act out what they saw happening in their dreams. In this way, Perls believed that by reliving the dream, the dreamer would *feel* what the message that was coming from his/her own unconscious mind really meant. For him, a dream was a 'signpost' giving directions along the path of a person's life.

Dream work in the 20th century

Since those early beginnings when Freud first took a psychological approach to dream interpretation, research into this subject has gone from strength to strength. What has been particularly exciting has been the scientific investigation into the whole mechanism of sleep. This really began in the middle of the 1950s, when scientists set up the first sleep laboratories, and what they have discovered as a result has not only been fascinating, but has revolutionized our understanding of what happens when we sleep.

In the dream laboratories, volunteers were wired up to a machine called an electroencephalograph, or EEG for short, so that researchers could measure the brain waves of the subjects as they slept. (Don't ask how these people managed to get a wink of sleep with all those wires attached to their heads – but miraculously, they did!) As well as the brain wave patterns, the laboratory equipment measured the volunteers' heartbeat, bloodpressure, temperature, breathing, muscular movements and all sorts of other body responses. The researchers monitored the machines and watched their subjects very carefully throughout the night.

By examining the changes in the brain wave patterns of their sleeping volunteers, the researchers found that we all go through four different stages of sleep from light to deep to very deep and up to light sleep again. It takes about one and a half hours to go through all these stages and the whole process repeats itself over and over again until we finally wake up. Throughout these different stages, our body responses change too, and the most fascinating physical response that the researchers observed was that during the lighter stages of sleep, the eyeballs of the volunteers started to roll around beneath their closed eyelids. They called this stage REM, or rapid-eye-movement sleep.

If the subjects were woken up during these REM periods, they were able to tell the researchers not only that they were dreaming but they could also recall exactly what they were dreaming about. But if they were woken up at other times, the subjects couldn't remember a thing. The researchers concluded that it is during the REM periods of lighter sleep that we dream. The researchers were then able to time precisely how long the eyeballs continue to flicker at any one time and this told them how long the dreams lasted. They also woke their volunteers at various times during their sleep and wrote down all the dreams they recounted.

This sort of research has been going on since the middle of this century, so you can imagine how many thousands of dreams have been collected in that time. It has been by studying all this material that researchers have discovered so much information about our dreams – how long each dream lasts, for example, the different types of dreams that we have and the most common things we dream about. And by matching the dreams to the events taking place in the lives of their volunteers, dream researchers have been able to piece together what the things we dream about actually mean.

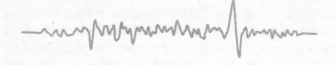

Chapter 2

Dreams

The mysterious imagery of your dreams

Making sense of your dreams

> *Question:* How can you tell an elephant was in your
> fridge?
> *Answer:* Because of the footprints in the butter.

Groan! How many times have you heard that joke before? It
must be as old as the hills and it hasn't improved with age.
Yes, it is ridiculous. But hold on a minute: if we stop to
think about it, it's no more ridiculous, stupid or absurd than
any of the dreams we have. So let's pretend it *is* a dream
and let's see if we can make any sense out of it. Let's
pretend that last night you had a dream that an elephant was
inside your fridge and that he left his footprints in the butter.

Elephants never forget

We know of course that an elephant couldn't possibly fit
into a fridge – well, not an ordinary kitchen-sized fridge,
that is. But to our unconscious minds that's just a trivial
detail. If a dream requires a jumbo to be stuffed into a
fridge, then stuff it in it will.

Ditto the elephant's footprints in the butter.

Now, why might you dream about an elephant anyway?
Well, at this stage you would have to ask yourself what an
elephant means to you. What do you think about when this
image comes into your head? Do you have any memories
or recollections of being near an elephant, feeding him
buns at the zoo, perhaps? Or did you do a project on
endangered species once and found that elephants
particularly fascinated you? Perhaps yesterday your friend
told you her mother had started going to Weight Watchers

31

because she'd put on so much weight over Christmas and her mum said she thought she'd turned into an elephant overnight. Or perhaps on the way home from school you bought a video of Walt Disney's *Dumbo* for your little sister's birthday tomorrow.

The possibilities are endless and as if that weren't enough, there are loads of sayings that we also associate with elephants, any of which could have sparked off this dream. For example, elephants are grey, they've got very thick skins, they've got long trunks, and they've got a reputation for never forgetting.

Finding the link

There's an amazing list of associations, and probably, if you keep thinking about it, you could come up with a couple of dozen more. Now think of each one of these as a piece of a jigsaw puzzle. What you have to do is pick out the piece that fits not only the rest of the dream but, more importantly, that also fits *your* thoughts, *your* memories, the events that have happened in *your* life, either quite recently or possibly even a long time ago, that have something to do with elephants.

So the next bit of the puzzle is the fridge. Now we've got to start all over again searching through all the possible meanings, associations, memories that you might have inside your head about fridges. Fridges might, for example, bring to mind things like cold, ice, white, box, food, kitchen, defrost and lots more besides.

Ditto the butter.

Free association

You can go on doing this for every image in your dream. It's called free association and it can be great fun. You can go off on all sorts of tangents and you'd be surprised what kind of weird and wonderful connections you can come up with for each image. Sooner or later you'll come across an association that goes 'ping!'. And that will be the very piece of the jigsaw puzzle that fits.

So, let's now pick out some of those associations and put them together in order to explain this dream.

> The elephant is a large animal.
> The fridge is a container of food.
> The butter is a fat.

Now, remember that conversation you had with your friend yesterday at break? She told you about her mum who said she'd got fat like an elephant. Her mum had overindulged at Christmas and Christmas is traditionally the time of year we associate with lots of food. We keep food in the fridge, so the fridge in your dream symbolizes food. Butter is made from fat; not only do we keep that in the fridge too, but it's also high in calories and too much of it can make people put on weight.

The punch line

OK, but why the footprints? Well, we can apply a bit of free association to the footprints as well. For example:

> We can follow in someone else's footprints.
> We leave footprints behind.
> Footprints can show us the way to go.

Again, we could think of lots more, but what seems to fit the dream imagery nicely here is the idea of leaving our footprints behind and, in effect, that's just what your friend's mum is going to do. She's going to turn her back on the high-calorie foods like butter which make her fat, so, in dream language, she's leaving her footprints behind her in the butter. And that is the final punch line of the dream.

Messages from your unconscious

So you see, your dreams are formed from your own personal experiences and from memories and impressions that come from deep inside your own unconscious and, because of that, you're the only one who can accurately know what your dream is referring to. As you've just seen, an image such as an elephant, or a footprint, in one person's dream can mean quite a different thing in another person's dream..

Dream symbols

However, it's also true that, because we're all human and we all experience things more or less in the same way, there are certain images or symbols that mean roughly the same sort of thing to all of us. For example, water is wet for everybody, ice is cold, stones are hard for you as well as for me and for everyone else too. These images are symbols that have carried the same message to all men and women since – well, since men and women were first invented.

Dream images

These symbols are important in dreams because they're like codes, if you like, or you can think of them as a form of shorthand. They are common to everyone the whole world over and each one can represent a complex set of experiences in a single picture. Water, for example, in our dreams is said to represent our feelings and emotions. To see a still pool suggests that the dreamer is calm and contained. But to dream of a raging torrent might be describing someone who's furious about something.

Sometimes, though, one particular image can have lots of different meanings and getting the right interpretation will depend on the context of the dream. Take, for example, the colour red. Now red can represent fire and heat. Red is the life blood that runs through our veins. Red can stand for passion, for love as well as for anger. Red is the colour of warning and tells of danger. Furthermore, red is the universally recognized sign for STOP.

Dream dictionaries

That's why dream dictionaries can be very useful. They can decode the images for you and they can give you all the alternative meanings of each symbol too. They can also help to jog your memory. What you have to do when you look up a particular image is to choose the meaning that you think most suits what's going on in your dream and in your life at that time.

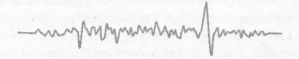

The key to understanding your dreams

But, the real key to understanding these messages from your unconscious is to ask yourself how you felt in the dream.

What emotions did you go through and how did you feel when you woke up?

If you're left feeling glad or elated, you know that the message is positive and encouraging. It's saying that things are OK for you at the moment. If you're left feeling sad, you need to look a little deeper into this dream to find what set off that sadness. There must have been an image or a situation in that dream that you associate with an upset. Ask yourself:

▶ Why did I have that sad dream?

▶ Did something happen yesterday that reminded me of a particular event in my life that made me unhappy?

▶ Did I watch a film that brought back an experience I've had in the past?

▶ Did someone say something that sparked off an old, painful memory?

Your sad dream is reminding you about an unhappy event and telling you whether or not that painful memory is getting better. If, after you wake up, you feel unhappy for a short while but soon brighten up again, it means that you are getting over it. But if the sad feelings last for longer, perhaps on and off throughout the day, then the emotional wound is still raw and you should talk it all through with someone, with your best mate, your mum, dad or someone sympathetic who is prepared to listen to you. Talking is a great healer.

Nightmares

It's the same for frightening dreams, for nightmares, or dreams that leave you feeling anxious or uneasy for the rest of the day. If fear is involved, then you really do need to put your finger on the problem. First, though, eliminate some obvious triggers, for example:

> ▶ Watching *Alien* or *Predator* before bed is enough to give anyone the heebie-jeebies, so it wouldn't be at all surprising to have a nightmare after that. (Why do we get such a thrill out of spooking ourselves silly?)
>
> ▶ Certain illnesses where you run a high fever are well-known causes of bad dreams.
>
> ▶ A big meal just before bed is often the culprit that triggers vivid, frightening dreams.

Under these kinds of conditions a nightmare is a way for your mind to discharge the fear or to alert you quickly to the physical discomfort that you're in. Perhaps you need to get a glass of water or take something for your indigestion.

But it's when that anxiety or that uneasiness stays with you that it pays to really work out the dream and to talk your fears through with someone, especially so if this sort of dream recurs.

The golden rule when it comes to analysing your dreams is to trust yourself and to listen to your own feelings. Think about what the images actually mean to you. Check each one out in the A-Z. Ask yourself what you associate that particular image with – whether it reminds you of an incident that has happened to you at some point in your life. You'll know when you've hit on the correct interpretation because it will *feel* right.

When it comes to understanding your dreams, follow your instincts and you will soon be unravelling the darkest, deepest, most fascinating workings of your unconscious mind.

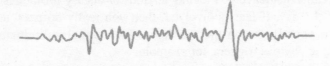

Six steps to help you analyse your dreams

1. Dream imagery: Write down your dream as soon as you can whilst it's still fresh in your mind. You'd be surprised how quickly the images vanish when you get into an argument with your brother about whose turn it is to get into the bathroom next! Once you've written down your dream, underline the most important images you remember seeing. Make a note of the colour, condition and anything else about these images that made them stand out.

2. Feelings and sensations: Try to remember the strongest feeling you had in the dream, write it down and draw a circle around it – e.g. did you feel frightened, happy, angry, hungry, cold, etc? Also, make a note of how you felt when you woke up. Don't cheat! If it made you blush, or feel embarrassed or ashamed of yourself, be honest and write it down.

3. Familiar faces and places: Did you recognize anybody or any places you know in your waking life? Was there anything different or unusual about these people or locations? For example, if you dreamt about your dad, was he wearing the clothes he normally wears or was he dressed as a clown, or in a strange uniform, or perhaps he was wearing a crown, or even a dress.

4. **Dream category:** Can you put your dream into a category or a theme – e.g. was it a dream about flying, falling, being chased, being late, being watched, to do with sex, being afraid of failure, being trapped, eating, travelling, meeting famous people? In short, what was it mostly about? You can find the ten most common dream themes on pages 13-15.

5. **Physical triggers:** Think if there might have been a physical cause to your dream – e.g. did you have too much to eat before you went to bed, were you cold in the night, did you have a pain, had you watched a thriller on TV just before bedtime, were you reading a horror story before you dropped off, if you're female had you just started your period, were you suffering from a bad cold and found it difficult to breathe? Any of these conditions could well be responsible for triggering a vivid dream.

6. **Background information:** What was going on in your waking life at the time that might have caused this type of dream – e.g. had you had a row with your best friend, were you moving or changing schools, were you in the middle of exams, had you just been out on a date with someone amazing, had your mum just won the lottery?

At this point, if you're not sure of the meaning behind any of the main images, colours, themes or whatever, look them up in the A-Z and jot that meaning down in the margin. Don't forget, an image may have several different meanings, so it's up to you to choose the one that you think best fits your dream and your personal circumstances. Trust yourself because only *you* are really the best judge of your own dreams.

Here is a real life example:

Kirstie's dream

I dreamt I was **snow-boarding** *but instead of sliding down the slope,* **I was going uphill.** *The funny thing was, I was going backwards so* **I couldn't see where I was going** *but I knew I was going up to the top and that everything was all right. It was so exciting and I was going really fast. On either side of the slope I could see* **green fields** *and* **gardens** *full of trees and flowers. It was a terrific dream and it made me feel great every time I thought about it throughout the following day.*

Background information: Kirstie had this dream soon after she entered Year 12 at school. She had successfully passed her exams and was now embarking on her A-level courses. She chose snow-boarding as her PE option and had had half a dozen lessons prior to this dream.

Interpretation: Snow-boarding is not only a sport but also a means of travel, so this dream is about movement and dreams that involve any form of movement and travel tell us something about the dreamer's progress in life. Here, Kirstie is travelling uphill so this represents ambition: she's moving towards the top which means she's aiming for achievement and success. In waking life she's recently done very well in her exams but now she's aiming higher, she's taking the next step and is studying for the next level. In the dream, though she's travelling uphill she's actually facing down, so the message here is that, whilst she can see what she has already achieved so far, she can't as yet see what exactly lies ahead of her. However, she *is* feeling confident, she's enjoying herself, and the green fields and gardens are endorsing this feeling of well-being. So, she knows she's doing well and that she's going in the right direction even though she doesn't know where that might lead. The dream was exciting and it made her feel great. It confirmed that she had made the right decisions in her life so far and that her future was looking good.

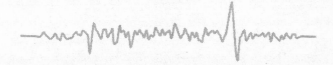

Happy dreaming and long may your dreams work for you.

Chapter 3

Dreams

The A-Z of dreams

Dreams

44

Abandoned

Dreaming that you've been left behind, that you're the only person on a desert island, that you're lost or all alone is fairly common especially when you're going through a period in your life when you feel lonely. For example, you might have this sort of dream after quarrelling and breaking up with your friends or when you feel left out or misunderstood.

Marie's dream

I was going shopping with my **mum** *around the grounds of* **my old primary school** *and I ran round the corner to look into a shop window. When I ran back to find my mum,* **the whole area was deserted and I couldn't see her anywhere.** *I was very upset and ran round and round calling for her.*

Category: fear and panic, sense of being all alone. Nightmare!

Interpretation: By setting the scene around her old primary school, this dream takes Marie back to when she was little. Being with her mother gives her a sense of security but when she loses her mother, she becomes very upset because she feels lost and isolated. An incident just like this actually did happen to Marie when she was four and she became separated for a few minutes from her mother in a busy store. But Marie is nearly sixteen now, so it's unlikely that she would get upset if this sort of thing happened to her these days. So why should she dream about the anxieties of being separated from her mother now? To answer this we need to look at what is happening to her at the moment. In fact, Marie has a big decision to make. She's very talented and wants to go to art college. She's been offered a place but the college is sixty miles away and if she takes the place it would mean living in digs all week and coming home only at weekends. This effectively means leaving home and Marie finds that a bit scary. But it's also exciting too. Alternatively, of course, she could stay on into the sixth form and stay at home. That's safe, but perhaps not so exciting. Her dream is now recalling that fear she felt when she lost her mother and was all on her own. Her unconscious mind is using this to bring Marie's attention to her present anxieties about leaving home, becoming independent and having to look after herself. Moreover, in the dream she's 'running round and round' and this mirrors the arguments running *round and round* in her head about what she should do – go to college or stay at home. This is a classic abandonment dream which lots of people have when they are going through major changes in their lives and when they are unsure of themselves and of what the future holds.

Accident

What sort of an accident is it, where does it happen and who's involved? It's important to tease out all the images in this dream in order to interpret it correctly. If you crash while you're running, cycling or driving, your unconscious may be telling you that you need to slow down in your waking life, that you're going too fast or doing too much. Or perhaps it could be a warning dream, alerting you to possible danger and you should take care when you're out over the next day or so. If your vehicle is out of control or if you're run over, your dream might be telling you that you're in a situation which you can't control. If you recognize your home as the scene of the accident, you may be worried about someone in your family. If it takes place at your school or college, you're probably anxious about your work or about a relationship with a teacher or a friend.

About sleep
In an average lifetime, a person spends over 200,000 hours asleep.

Actor

If you dream of an actor, think of performance, drama and illusion and then ask yourself if someone you know isn't being as genuine as he/she makes out. Perhaps a person is trying to pull the wool over your eyes. Alternatively, dreaming about being on stage, or with actors, or celebrities or members of the royal family, can symbolize that you have a strong need to be noticed.

Admiration

Who's doing the admiring and what, or who, is being admired? To dream that someone is admiring you can mean that you're confident about your appearance or your talents and that soon you can expect praise for your efforts. Perhaps, too, this is telling you that you'll soon get a wish granted. It's said that if you're the one who's admiring another person, it's a sign that you're attracting luck your way. If you're admiring someone else's girl/boyfriend, though, it might be because you have eyes on that person in real life. But if it's an object rather than a person that is being admired, you need to work out the symbolism behind that thing. For example, are you admiring a ring? If so, you may be secretly yearning for a boy or girlfriend of your

47

own because a ring symbolizes relationships. But if you're admiring a bird flying high in the sky, you may be wishing that you could get better marks in your school work because a bird represents ambition.

Adventure

A dream where you're having an exciting adventure may have been triggered off by a horror movie you watched before going to bed and now your unconscious is replaying it back to you in your dream – except that this time *you're* in the starring role. The important thing here is whether you were excited or terrified throughout your adventure. If you were having a whale of time, you may actually need to do something a bit more challenging in real life. Perhaps you secretly yearn to take up an energetic sport, snow-boarding for example, rock climbing or orienteering? If your dream adventure frightened the pants off you, though, you need to ask yourself whether you're doing something in your waking life that is likely to land you in hot water. This could be a warning to you not to take any risks.

Aeroplane

Flying in an aeroplane, like all dreams about flying, symbolizes confidence and ambition. The higher the plane goes, the more sure you are of yourself and the more 'high-flying' you would like to be. If you're the pilot, it means you're in charge and in control of things at the moment. If you're a passenger and the flight is bumpy, it could mean that something is going wrong in your life just now and you feel powerless, out of control or unable to put matters right. A dream where the aeroplane crashes may be drawing your attention to a lack of confidence and a fear of failure.

Aliens

There are currently so many films and books about extra-terrestrials and flying saucers that it's not surprising to learn that dreams about aliens are now fairly common and simply replay in the sleeping mind what was seen on the television or at the cinema during the day. However, because aliens, and indeed all foreigners, are strange to us and speak in a language we don't understand, dreaming about them suggests that we are confused or uncertain about something that is happening in our lives at the moment. For example, you might have this sort of dream when you move house and find yourself in a new neighbourhood or when you change schools and everything around you is different and unfamiliar.

Alley

This is a very important dream symbol because alleyways, paths, roads, passageways, corridors or streets all represent your journey and progress in life. Walking or running down the alley in your dream is like a mirror of you going about your daily affairs in your waking life. How do you feel as you walk down that alleyway? If you're quite confident and not bothered, it means that life is OK for you at present, you're happy with your friends and your work is under control. But if you're afraid, frightened of what's lurking in the shadows, it may mean that you lack self-confidence or that you're afraid of something or someone in your life.

Dream researchers have found that people can train themselves to control the action of their dreams, so that if you're afraid of something, for example, you can make yourself confront whatever it is, shout at it, chase it, throw stones at it and drive it away. To do this you need to tell yourself before you fall asleep that if you have a scary dream, you want to be able to take control of things, or to have a happy ending. This is particularly valuable if you suffer from recurring nightmares. Psychologists suggest that if you have a bad dream, you should try to doze off again, all the while thinking pleasant thoughts, and then pick up the dream where it left off, but this time invent a better ending. Alternatively, if you can't get back to sleep, think the dream right through again but add whatever ending to it you want. This will help you to overcome whatever difficulties lie in store in your waking life.

The condition of the alley is also important in this dream. For example, if it's dark and full of dirty rubbish, it might mean that you think life is a bit of a mess just now. If there's a deadend, could it be that you've got a difficult problem you can't resolve in your waking hours? Perhaps there's an open gateway or light coming through an opening in the wall. If so, that could be a way out for you, so your dream is telling you that if you look further into this problem, or work harder, you will find an answer. If you're running hell-for-leather through the alley, your unconscious might be telling you to slow down, to take things easy, not to rush around so much. A dream where you're squeezing yourself through a tight, narrow alley is associated with pressure to get something done in time in your real life.

Altar

We associate altars with places of sacrifice, so to dream of one may be hinting that you have a tendency to 'sacrifice' yourself or your needs for the sake of others. In other words, do you generally go along with your mates, or do what *they* want to do, instead of doing what *you* want to do? So do you feel put upon? Do you stand up for yourself, for your rights and beliefs or do you give in easily just to please other people? Whilst it's good to be kind and considerate to others, this dream may be prompting you to take a look at yourself, suggesting that you might be a bit of a pushover, easily influenced or playing the role of a martyr or victim in your life at the moment.

About sleep
When your mother tells you you need your beauty sleep, she's absolutely right because it's whilst we're asleep that our bodies heal and repair themselves.

Amusement arcade

An amusement arcade suggests fun, and that is perhaps what this dream is telling you, that life is great for you right now. If you're winning at the machines, your unconscious may be confirming how talented and skilful you are. But if you're losing and you keep putting lots of money into the slot machines, it may be a warning to you that you're getting yourself into a no-win situation in real life and that no matter how much effort you put into it, you simply won't succeed. This dream is telling you to quit while you're ahead.

Angel

Take note of what an angel gives you or says to you in a dream because they act as messengers, bringing you important information from deep inside your unconscious, or else they tell you news of things to come. Their other role, of course, is that of protector or guardian angel. To see an angel in your dream, then, is telling you that someone, or something, is protecting you in your waking life.

51

Dreams

Animals

Dreams in which animals appear can be interpreted in several ways. Firstly, if you have a pet, it can figure as itself, simply as the kitten or the puppy that you love so much. Secondly, animals can take the place of someone we know: a good mate in your dream might be represented by a dog because we say that dogs are 'man's best friend'. Or a bear might substitute for a grumpy teacher. Thirdly, old dream books say that animals appearing in our dreams may be messengers or guardians, so that we should take note of what they do, or listen carefully to what they tell us. And if we're going through a difficult patch in our lives, dreaming of an animal might be reassuring us that we are somehow protected, we're being looked after and we shouldn't worry because, one way or another, things will work out right. Finally, individual animals symbolize particular qualities so that to dream of an owl, for example, tells us something about wisdom, a lion may be interpreted as courage or a chicken as cowardice. Look up individual animals under their alphabetical listing.

Ants

Because ants are hard-working insects, dreaming about them may be confirming what a busy, industrious person you are. To see an ant's nest or colony might be symbolizing your school, your block of flats or any other place you know that is teeming with life and activity. Seeing ants crawling all over you is warning you that little things are likely to irritate you or to get on your nerves in the next couple of days. Perhaps you're being a bit over-sensitive.

Apple >

Is the apple sweet or sour? Is it ripe and shiny or lying brown and rotten on the ground? To dream of sweet, ripe, shiny apples is a good omen that might signify good fortune coming your way. Rotten apples lying on the floor and going to waste could symbolize your wasted efforts. Perhaps this dream is suggesting that you could make the best of your abilities if you worked harder and didn't squander your talents. This would be particularly true if there were some lovely red apples still on the tree telling you that you still have masses of potential.

Arm >

Dream analysts have found that occasionally people who have something wrong with a part of their body, say an infection in their lungs, for example, dream about that area of their anatomy. Our unconscious minds are quite able to prompt us about our health and will point out areas that need attention. If we take heed of these dreams, we could see the doctor and get cured before the illness becomes very serious. On a different level, we use our arms to hug and hold people we love, so to dream of putting your arms around someone means you want to get closer to that person, or to give him or her your affection. To dream that a person puts his/her arms around you implies that you need to be loved and protected. Who is it who's putting his/her arms around you? That's the sixty-four thousand dollar question...

Arrow

Although arrows are essentially weapons, symbolically they become pointers, travelling in the direction of a target. To see an arrow flying may represent an idea, an ambition or a solution to a problem. Where the arrow lands could hold the answer to that problem; could point the direction you should be taking in life or show you the outcome of that idea. If you shoot the arrow but it misses the target, your unconscious may be trying to tell you that your efforts are falling on stony ground or that you're working towards the wrong goal. As Cupid's darts, of course, arrows will symbolize your feelings of love. If you're struck by one, you've probably fallen for someone in real life. If *you're* shooting Cupid's arrow at a person, it may be someone you fancy and you want him or her to fall in love with you. Alternatively, if you're shooting an arrow and in the dream you feel angry and aggressive towards someone, it means you've got a grudge against that person in real life. If you're badly wounded by an arrow, it's possible you're being warned that someone will upset you.

Artist

Dreaming about an artist or seeing yourself painting a picture is an expression of your creativity and here your unconscious is encouraging you to paint or sketch or draw. This dream is saying: you're talented, you're artistic, you can do it, go on, go for it.

Attack

To dream that you're being attacked may be a direct warning, telling you to be careful and to take care of yourself. This dream is probably a reflection of worries or feelings of paranoia that you may have been experiencing in your waking life. Perhaps your unconscious is advising you not to put yourself in a situation or place of danger. Or, this dream could be alerting you that you're in for a bout of ill health since, for example, when we catch a cold we are 'attacked' by viruses. But apart from a physical attack, this dream may be suggesting that you're about to come in for some verbal abuse. Perhaps someone will criticize you unfairly or you might quarrel and fall out with a friend. If you're the one who's doing the attacking, however, your unconscious is trying to release some hidden anger. Who is it that you're attacking? If it's someone you know, it could mean that you're feeling resentful towards him/her. If you see someone being attacked and you step in to help the victim, or you manage to stop the attack altogether, it means that you may be able to solve whatever problem that is worrying you in your waking life.

B

Baby

Babies symbolize your ideas or your own potential gifts and talents. A baby can also represent a project that you want to work on and giving birth to a baby means you're ready to start. If you feel great love for the baby then you're enjoying what you're doing. Happy babies are usually a sign that you're feeling contented and secure. But if the baby cries and annoys you, the dream is telling you that you're frustrated with what's going on in your waking life or that your project or idea is not working out well. A tiny baby or one that's born prematurely could be a warning that your idea hasn't been thought through properly and that you need to spend more time on it to get things right. This dream is telling you not to give up but that if you concentrate on what you're doing you'll get good results. It's also saying keep on going as you are, don't make any changes because the time isn't right to start anything new yet. However, if the baby grows and takes a few steps, that's the signal for you to move on to something new.

Did you know that:
you began to dream even before you were born, when you were still snug and warm inside your mother's womb.

Bag

Bags and baggage make fascinating dream symbols and can be interpreted in several ways depending on the rest of the action in the dream. On a superficial level, if you see a row of suitcases, it could mean that you're on the move or that you'll be going on a journey soon. Perhaps it's coming to the end of term or else you might be off on your holidays in the next few days. But because bags are containers into which we put things, under the lore of dream these can symbolize the problems and responsibilities that we carry around with us in our everyday lives. So, if you dream that you're carting about a really heavy bag, it might be that you're feeling overburdened by a real-life problem, or perhaps you feel you have too many responsibilities. This is particularly so if the bag in your dream resembles the one you take to school every day. If it is, it might be that you're finding school a bit of a drag just now. Of course, if you're happily carrying your school bag and it doesn't feel heavy or uncomfortable, it suggests that life at school is fine. If you open a bag and find it contains money, jewellery or other valuables, your dream may be telling you that you have terrific talents. Or perhaps you might soon learn something important, something that will be of value to you in the future. This dream, however, may have a completely different interpretation altogether because, according to some dream specialists, a bag can be the symbol for a woman's uterus or vagina so this dream could have a sexual meaning to it. Other images in the dream will give you a clue as to its true meaning, but if it is an 'erotic' dream, you need to look up the section on **Sex** for further information.

Ball – as in football

Dreaming about ball games can have many interesting meanings. For example, are you playing in a team or on your own? If you're a team member and you're playing football, hockey, cricket or whatever, your dream is telling you something about how well you're cooperating in real life with the people around you, like your family and school mates. Are you winning or losing? Winning shows you're getting on well. Losing suggests things aren't going so well for you at the moment. If you're the one who scores a goal or hits the ball for six, you're probably enjoying a spell of popularity in your waking life, or else you can expect a special merit or praise or a success of some kind. But if you were responsible for missing a goal, you might be feeling guilty because you let someone down. If in your dream, you're playing all on your own, kicking a football against a wall, let's say, this might mean that you're feeling lonely and left out of things just now. On quite a different level, because we refer to male testicles as balls, a dream of this kind may have a sexual meaning, especially so if you

57

see two balls together, say two golf balls lying on a green, or two billiard balls on a snooker table. Perhaps if you're female this dream, then, may be referring to a boy you know – or would like to get to know...
(See also Sex.)

Ball – as in dance

To be dancing at a Cinderella-type glittering ball suggests that your life is great at the moment and that you're having fun, having a ball, in fact. Are you the belle of the ball? Alternatively, perhaps you have a great desire to be noticed or wish you were more popular. If everyone else is dancing except you, you're probably feeling left out and miserable in real life at present.

Bat – the animal kind

In dream lore, as in real life, bats don't get a good press. To dream of one may be an omen of bad news. Also remember the expression, 'blind as a bat'. Perhaps if you dream of this your unconscious is telling you that you're not seeing the whole picture, or that you're not wanting to face the truth, or that someone is trying to deceive you.

Bat – the sort used in cricket

Playing a bat and ball game in your dream, such as cricket or tennis, means that you're concerned about your abilities and skills. If you're winning you can be reassured that you do have talent and that you're bound to succeed in whatever you set your mind to do. If you're losing, though, it might mean that in real life it's time to put in some more practice or even to have a rethink.

Bath ▷

Whenever water figures in your dreams, it's an almost sure bet that your unconscious is telling you something about your emotional state of mind. So, seeing water running into a bath can mean you have a problem or an upset that needs sorting out. If the water is clean and scented with bath salts, it means you've got a clear conscience and will be able to work out the problem. But if the water is scummy and dirty, you need to ask yourself whether you've contributed to the problem you're facing, or made matters worse: perhaps you're not entirely squeaky clean. Or perhaps it means that the problem is confusing or complicated and there doesn't seem to be any clear solution. If you're in the bath and you're washing or scrubbing yourself vigorously, it means you're trying to wash away your troubles. If you're washing your hands, it may mean that you don't want to have anything more to do with a certain person or with a particular situation in your waking life – you want to 'wash your hands' of the whole affair.

Beach ▷

Most people have fun at the seaside, so dreaming about lazing or messing about on the beach is a reminder of fun and games. If you're sunbathing on the beach, your unconscious may be telling you it's time to relax more, spend time on your hobbies or take up a new interest. If you're walking all alone on the beach without a single person in sight, you may be feeling lonely or left out at this time in your life: perhaps you're missing your friends or someone special you really care for. But if you stand and look out to sea, it means you're ready to face a new challenge, you're ready to start again. Of course, being at the beach means that you're close to the sea, and water is linked to our feelings. If the sea is turbulent, you could be upset about something. But if it's calm, then so are you.

Bear

Animals in our dreams either represent someone we know or a situation that is happening to us in real life. Or it might be that it's the characteristics of that animal that we should be taking note of. For example, we tend to think of bears as grisly and bad-tempered. So if you know someone who's always grumpy and cross, he or she may appear in your dreams in the form of a bear. If *you're* the bear in the dream, you may need to question whether you've been acting a bit aggressively lately.

Teddy bears, however, have quite a different meaning because, as our childhood toys, we love them and treat them like best friends. To dream of a teddy bear, then, may be reminding you of things you used to do when you were little. Or perhaps it means you need cuddling and comforting. In a girl's dream a teddy bear may represent her boyfriend, especially if he's got brown hair and is really cuddly!

Bed

Have you been burning the candle at both ends recently, staying up late and generally not getting enough beauty sleep? If so, you may well dream about a bed – a whacking great hint from your unconscious telling you that you're tired and it's about time you had an early night. Beds can also symbolize comfort, as well as our privacy and security. If you've had a difficult day and perhaps have been feeling a bit got at, you may dream of your bed that night, because that's where you feel safe and warm. Sometimes you might dream that you're in a strange bed in a room you don't recognize. This may be anticipating a move: perhaps you'll be staying over at a friend's house soon, or maybe going off on holiday. But of course beds can also have a sexual link and to dream that you're making the bed may be a sign that you're ready for a new relationship.

Bee

Like ants, bees are industrious creatures, so to dream of a bee buzzing around is telling you that you may soon be as busy as a bee. In ancient times bees were regarded as lucky omens and to dream of one was said to bring happiness and good fortune. But if you're stung by a bee in your dream, beware. This is said to be a sign of treachery and could mean that someone will let you down.

Hari's dream

A **bee** *was under* **my pillow** *and it* **tried to sting me** *but* **I held it** *and though* **it was buzzing around me** *I was surprised that* **it didn't sting** *me after all.*

Interpretation: Bees are industrious creatures, so to see them in a dream going about their business, flying from flower to flower collecting their pollen usually suggests that the dreamer is going through a busy spell in his or her life. The pillow immediately takes us to Hari's bed, a place where he rests. The bee is under the pillow, thus putting the hard work and the rest together side-by-side. What this dream is suggesting is that Hari has some work to do but he would prefer not to do it. On questioning him about this, he admits he has a history project which needs to be handed in soon and he hasn't done a stroke of work on it yet. In the dream, Hari grabs the bee and holds it. This is his unconscious mind encouraging him to make a start on the work, just to grit his teeth and get on with it. The bee buzzes around him which is probably annoying and irritating just as the thought of the project is annoying and irritating for him, too. But, in fact, Hari's unconscious is telling him that when he actually gets going, he's going to be surprised to find quite how interesting this project will turn out. In dream language, he will discover that the bee doesn't sting him at all!

Beetle

In ancient Egypt beetles, and in particular the scarab beetle, were considered emblems of good luck and long life. So dreaming of this insect can be a good omen as long as you don't feel afraid or disgusted by it. If there are lots of swarming bugs or beetles around you, this dream may be warning you that you'll have some irritations to put up with in the next few days.

Being chased *(See Running.)*

Bells

Quite often, noises that are going on in the world around us whilst we are sound asleep are picked up by our unconscious and are woven into a dream. Bells are typical of this and are commonly dreamt of early in the morning, seconds before we wake up to find the alarm clock going off, or the postman ringing at the door.

Bike

Because it takes a lot of personal effort to pedal a bike, a dream where you're cycling along represents the progress you're making in your life at present. If you're riding smoothly and happily, it's a sign of success. If you're cycling fast downhill, feel that you're out of control, fall off, or even crash, it may be a warning that you should take more care with your work or else you'll come a cropper.

Birds

In dreams birds are winged messengers, so think carefully about the information they are carrying. However, a dream where *you* are the bird soaring high in the sky tells you that you are feeling confident and reminds you of your high-flying ambitions. You might have this sort of dream when you've won a race or come top in a test. A bird singing sweetly in your dream is said to be a sign of good news to come.

Birthday

Birthdays in dreams can mark a time of fun and celebration or they can represent a new beginning and a fresh start, depending on the rest of the action in the dream and also, of course, on what's going on in your life at the time. If it is your birthday there may be a surprise in store. How many candles are there on the cake? The number may be very significant, so look it up under the entry for **Numbers**.

Blackboard

Is anything written on the blackboard? If there is, take note: this may be a message to you from your unconscious and you'll have to work out its meaning. Alternatively, this dream may simply be replaying something that happened to you at school that day, perhaps stressing an event that left an important impression on you. If the blackboard is blank, this could be a hint that you should be making your mark in some way, perhaps it's telling you to get on with some work or to develop your talents.

Blood

There are several meanings that can be applied to blood in a dream. Firstly, since it is essential to life, a dream where you are bleeding can suggest that for some reason you are being drained or losing your life energy, either because you're under stress or under the weather – perhaps you've caught a cold or 'flu. And because blood is red, it may simply be representing some of the things we associate with that colour, like heat, warmth, anger or passion. However, research has also shown that women often dream about blood each month just before they menstruate – almost as if their unconscious is giving them a little nudge and reminding them that they will soon be starting a period.

Boats

Ships, boats and sailing vessels of all kinds come under the category of transport and, according to dream lore, forms of moving transport (including seeing yourself walking or running) represent the progress you're making in your life. A smooth journey with nice scenery says that life's OK at the moment. So, if you dream of a boat gliding over a calm sea, it means that everything is 'plain sailing' for you in your waking life. The opposite is true if the boat is being buffeted about in rough seas on a stormy night. This suggests that you've got problems, perhaps having rows with your parents or breaking up with your friends. Remember that whenever water appears in your dreams, it's describing your current emotional state in real life. If a boat sinks, perhaps you've had one of your hopes dashed, or you may have to ditch a plan you'd had in mind. If you're on land and you're watching a boat sail away, you may be regretting a missed opportunity.

*(See also **Water**.)*

Did you know that:
when you were one-year-old you dreamed on and off for about five hours every day.

Body

If you dream about your head, your arm, your leg or any other bit of your anatomy, it may be a premonition. For example, if you see yourself rubbing your foot, it might be a sign that you'll be doing some activity where you could stub your toe or trip and sprain your ankle. Or else this dream might be about wishful thinking. For example, if you're female and in your dream you have big breasts, it might be because in real life you think your breasts are small and you really would love to have a chest like Pamela Anderson's. It's quite common to compensate in a dream for what we haven't got in our waking lives. So, a timid, gentle girl might see herself as a strong, confident lad in her dreams; someone who's afraid of the sea may become a champion swimmer; and someone who can't walk at all may dream of him/herself triumphantly playing football with his/her mates. In the symbolizm of dream language, however, particular parts of the body have their own significance. Dreaming of ears, for instance, may mean that you're not listening to what someone is trying to tell you, whilst dreaming of closed eyes could be warning you that someone is trying to deceive you.

Book

In general, books are good omens in your dreams and foretell happiness, especially if you're reading one. What's the book called and can you remember anything written in it? If so, this could be a message about something that is likely to happen. If you're writing in the book, it may be a reminder of something you have to do when you wake up – perhaps you need to finish off an essay for school. If you're in a house filled with books, your dream is saying that you feel overloaded with work.

Box

Dreams in which boxes appear are fascinating because the message lies in whatever is contained inside the box. If the box is full of money or jewels, it may foretell that good luck is coming your way. Opening the box only to find it's empty could represent a disappointment. If the box is locked and you don't have the key, it suggests that there's some kind of mystery going on, or that there's something you don't understand. You can look up any objects inside the box under their alphabetical listing to find out the meaning behind one of these dreams. Also, look up **Sex** because in some dreams a box may be representing a woman's sexual organs.

Boyfriend

If you haven't got a boyfriend and you dream of meeting one, you'd be wise to keep your eyes open over the next few days as this could be a predictive dream. Dreaming that you're kissing a boyfriend suggests you need to be loved. Dreaming that you're kissing and cuddling means you're happy and feel loved. If your boyfriend is kissing another girl in your dream, it's likely you've picked up some clues in your waking life that make you suspicious about his loyalty to you. People in our dreams are often interchangeable, especially if we recognize characteristics that they have in common – if they stand in the same way, wear the same type of clothes, have similar smiles. So your real life boyfriend may, in your dream, look like your brother or a famous actor or the check-out boy in your local supermarket. What your unconscious is doing here is pointing out ways in which someone in your waking life is like the person in your dream. Other clues to the meaning of a dream about your boyfriend may be found in the clothes he is wearing – a red shirt could mean he is angry with you, because red conveys passion. If he's holding a map, it could be suggesting that he's going on a journey or perhaps it's a hint that he could be thinking of leaving you.

Bread

Whether in the form of a loaf, a roll or even a sandwich, as a staple food of life, to see fresh bread in your dreams is an omen of good luck, especially if you're eating it. Eating or sharing bread with other people is a sign that you'll be having fun with your friends. Mouldy bread, though, is a warning of lost opportunities, of relationships turning sour and generally of a miserable time ahead. If in your waking life you refer to money as 'bread', loaves or rolls in your dream will stand for cash. In this dream, if you give a roll or a sandwich away, it means you'll be spending or giving away money.

Bracelet

Finding a bracelet in your dreams is a sign of good luck. Losing a bracelet could mean that you're going to lose something valuable in your waking life.

Bride and bridegroom

If you've recently been to a wedding, it wouldn't be at all surprising to see a bride and bridegroom in your dream, because that would be your unconscious simply playing the event back to you in your sleep. If you're the bride, you may be having a dream of wishful thinking, especially if you've got a steady boyfriend that you really care for. Otherwise, seeing brides, bridegrooms and weddings in general may be a sign that you'll soon be making big changes in your life like, for example, leaving school and going to college.

Bridge

This is an important dream symbol because a bridge is a walkway and, like all other walkways (e.g. paths, roads, alleyways etc), this represents your progress through life. The interesting thing about a bridge is that, unlike a road, it carries people safely over rivers, railway tracks, motorways, or other similar dangers. Stepping onto the bridge means that you're about to go through a change in your life. If you're crossing the bridge, your unconscious is confirming that you're on the right track and that you've avoided some kind of danger in your life. For example, if someone in your waking life has been urging you to do something you believe is wrong and you've refused to do it, this dream is telling you that you made the right decision. If you see the bridge but you're too afraid to cross it, it means that you're puzzled about something and you're not sure what to do. If you cross the bridge and step off the other side, it means that you've successfully resolved a problem, or that you've conquered a fear or come through a difficult patch in your life. The stronger the bridge and the more confident you are about crossing it, the more able you will be to cope with any problems you may have in your waking life.

Broom

Are you trying to sweep something under the carpet? If this is what you're doing in your dream, perhaps you've done something in your waking life that you want to sweep away, or to cover over. Or maybe, like the saying 'a new broom sweeps clean', this dream is telling you it's time to make a fresh start, especially if you're sweeping stuff out of the door. Perhaps it's time for you to have a clear-out, or put a stop to old, negative habits. Or maybe it's time to finish with an old relationship, to make way for a new one?

Brother

Much depends on how you actually feel about your brother as to how you should interpret this dream. If you usually get along well, then it's a sign of reassurance, a signal that all is well in your life. If, though, you fight like cats and dogs, this dream may represent rows or upsets or bad feelings. Brothers, of course, may be symbolizing males outside of the family, so that whilst you're seeing your brother in a dream, he may actually be standing in for a boyfriend or someone you fancy. Although this might make you go 'euuuukkkk' when you wake up and realize the connection, it's quite common for our unconscious minds to substitute people and places in our dreams: it's like taking a short-cut or writing in shorthand, so don't be surprised if your unconscious plays this trick on you!

Bucket

Like a box, a bucket is a container, so it's important to notice what is in it. If the bucket contains water, your dream is trying to tell you something about your feelings. Since water is linked to emotions, if the water is clean, you're calm and happy, in control of what's going on in your life. But if the water is dirty or muddy, it could be that you're upset, or you can't quite work out how you feel about something or someone. If there are rocks in your bucket, you may be going through a difficult time, and if the bucket is heavy as well, it's likely that you feel weighed down by your problems.

Bugs

Something is likely to 'bug' you, or there could be a few 'bugs' in the system. Either way, dreaming of bugs is a warning that things are likely to annoy or irritate you over the next few days.

Burglary

This is a fear dream because although theft of any sort is unpleasant, a burglary in particular leaves us feeling violated. A house symbolizes your body, so to dream of your house being burgled may mean that you're worried about being attacked in some way. You might have this dream if in real life, for example, you're afraid of bullies, or if you've been physically threatened by somebody. If you do have this sort of dream under these circumstances, it would be worth talking your problems through with a sympathetic adult. This dream might alternatively imply that someone has said something nasty about you and unjustly blackened your reputation. But, of course, there's also the possibility that this dream is alerting you to the lack of security you have in your house, which could make it an easy target for burglars. Let your parents know about these anxieties: they may take extra precautions from now on and make sure they lock all the doors and windows.

Did you know that:
by the time you're twenty, you'll be lucky if you get as much as two hours' worth of dream time in one night.

Burial

It's not unusual to experience a feeling of suffocation or to dream that you're being buried alive, if you've had a big meal just before going bed. At other times, you might have this sort of dream if you get tangled up in your bedclothes or if your duvet feels heavy on you while you're asleep. Generally, though, dreams of burial and death aren't half as dreadful as they sound. They should not be taken as a prediction that someone will die, but rather as a prediction of change.. So, if you see yourself being buried in your dream, it means the end of one chapter in your life and the beginning of something new.

Bus

We all know the joke about waiting hours for a bus and then

finding that two or three come along at the same time. Well, buses in dreams are like opportunities – you can hang around for ages waiting for the right opening and then, just when you're fed up, two or three offers come your way all at once. If you dream that you catch a bus, it means you won't miss any opportunities coming your way. If you miss the bus, your dream is telling you that you've blown your chances.

Butterfly

You've heard of a butterfly mind. Perhaps seeing a butterfly flitting about from flower to flower in your dream may be a hint that you're a bit fickle or that you're frittering away your talents or your energies. Another aspect of this insect is that it changes shape, it transforms itself from a drab chrysalis into a gloriously beautiful winged creature. Bearing this in mind, then, your dream may be telling you it's time for your own transformation – a new-look you – whether that means changing your image (perhaps doing your hair differently) or swapping any negative or immature habits for more grown-up behaviour. Also, because these are such gorgeous creatures, this dream may be telling you to have beautiful thoughts, to be more colourful and more creative. And if you think it's the colour of the butterfly that stands out in your dream, find out what that colour means by looking it up under the section on **Colour**.

Cage

Are you feeling trapped or cooped up in your life? If so, that's just what this dream is reflecting. If the cage door is open, though, your unconscious is telling you the situation isn't all gloom and doom, because there is a way out. To dream of a cage full of birds traditionally means good luck is heading your way. If there are only two birds in the cage, it's a sign of a happy relationship.

Cake

To dream of cakes and other forms of confectionery is very favourable and usually means that you're in for a good time.

Candle

Candles lighten the darkness, so to dream of one suggests hope and improvement in some way. Remember, where there's light, there's hope. If you've had a difficult problem on your mind, seeing yourself lighting a candle in your dream will mean that you'll find the solution soon. If you blow out the candle, you may be wanting to put an end to a certain situation – or a certain relationship – in your life. If the candle sputters or is blown out by the wind, a disappointment may be in store. On a different level, because of their long, thin shape, candles can also be taken as a phallic symbol, so to dream of one may suggest you're feeling sexy.

Car

When you dream of a car, think of it as representing your energy and what 'drives' you to do the things that you do. If, in your dream, you're driving along and enjoying the ride, it means you're doing well and are happy in your waking life. If there are problems with the car and it won't go or it breaks down, this could be a message that you're not using your talents to the best of your ability, or that you're just wasting your time and your energy. Crashing a car suggests that things are getting out of control in your life. What kind of car is it? Is it a shiny new one or a clapped out old banger? A shiny one in great condition shows you're on top of things, but one that's just an old heap of rust suggests you've let things slip and it's time you did something to improve your image and your style.

Castle

To dream of a beautiful castle is a good omen of riches or opportunities to come. If you're inside a fortress-like castle, you're feeling safe and secure in your life at the moment. A ruined castle suggests that your plans could be spoilt. Or is the castle surrounded by clouds? If so, this can imply that you're building castles in the air, which means you're being unrealistic and your hopes and dreams may not come true.

Cat

Firstly, you need to ask yourself how you feel about cats. Do you love them or loathe them? Do you think of them as friendly, furry bundles of fun or as scheming, cunning creatures who always manage to get the cream? Historically, cats have had a bad press and have been linked to superstitions of bad luck and misfortune. In ancient Egypt, however, cats were revered because the Egyptians believed they had psychic powers. Nowadays, cats in dreams represent intuition and instincts, so to dream of one may be a device that the unconscious mind is using to encourage a dreamer to follow his or her hunches. Cats may also represent females, and one that attacks or scratches you in your dream may symbolize an enemy – someone who wants to get her claws into you.

Cave

A dream about a cave can have several interpretations depending on the rest of the action in the dream. Sometimes it can represent the dark recesses of the mind, the parts about ourselves that we don't fully understand or maybe the negative characteristics in our nature that we don't want to admit we possess. So, if you dream you're in a cave and you light it up with a torch, it means you're exploring your hidden talents: maybe it's a sign that you're beginning to develop some of your latent abilities. Take note of anything that may be written on the walls as this could be a message to you from your unconscious. Also, notice any objects in the cave as these may have a strong bearing on what's going on in your life at the moment. You can look up such objects under their alphabetical listing to find out what they mean and how they relate to this dream. If you're afraid to enter the cave, ask yourself what could be inside that you don't want to see. If it's a bear or a snake, for example, these symbolize your fears in life. For a boy, a cave may have a sexual meaning in his dream as it can represent a girl's vagina or, more generally, it can describe the sort of relationship he's having with his girlfriend. For example, if the cave is warm and cosy, his relationship is happy, but if the cave is cold and bleak, his girlfriend may be giving him a hard time. If he dreams that he is entering the cave, it means he wants to take his relationship further and get much more intimate with his girlfriend.
(See also Sex.)

CDs

It's a good omen if, in your dream, you're listening to groovy music but a bad omen if you hate the music you

75

hear. Music that you like means that you'll be getting exciting news. To hear discordant or jangly music, or a tune that drives you mad warns of arguments and disagreements. And if the music is definitely out of tune, could it be that your unconscious is hinting that *you* are 'out of tune' in some way, perhaps going through a phase when you're disagreeing with your parents or not fitting in with your mates? However, you can expect to have fun with your friends if you dream that you're putting a tape or CD on the hi-fi, especially if you're with a crowd. Dreaming that you're buying a CD is warning you not to be extravagant if you're out shopping.

Chain

To dream of a gold or silver chain is a good omen of luck, especially if someone gives you the chain as a present. To lose a chain, though, may mean that you're anxious about losing something precious – a boy/girlfriend, perhaps? This dream could be a gentle reminder, telling you to take better care of the people or things that you love. Historically, chains have been a symbol of oppression and slavery. If, then, you dream that you're bound up in chains, it means that you're frustrated, that you can't free yourself from a situation that's tying you down in your conscious life. If you dream that you're putting a chain around someone's neck, it means that you want to 'chain' that person to you, or that you want to control the relationship you have with him or her.

Chair

Dreaming of a soft, comfortable chair foretells good luck. Hard chairs suggest difficulties ahead. If the chair is old and tatty, it suggests you're feeling old-fashioned or out of

The A–Z of dreams

the swing of things, so it's time for you to update and get a new image. If you're moving a chair, or even throwing it out, it means you've been feeling overburdened with a problem, with your school work or with some other responsibilities and now it's time to offload.

> **Did you know that:**
> if you live into your 70s you will have spent about ten years of your life dreaming.

Chase

If you're running after someone, you need to ask yourself whether, in your real life, you're making a play for a particular person. Are you 'chasing after' him or her? If, on the other hand, *you're* the one who's being chased, look up **Running** under the alphabetical listing to find out what it means.

Chicken

Chickens are not particularly good news in dreams as they can be a warning that your hopes will be dashed, especially if you're actually eating the chicken, thus implying that you will spoil your own chances of success. On a different level, we say 'chicken' to someone who is being cowardly. Are you that chicken in your dream and, if so, do you think your unconscious is trying to tell you something about your behaviour?

Children

Children can represent future hopes and ambitions. To dream of a child and a parent together may be showing you a symbolic comparison between: immaturity vs maturity, youth vs old age, impotence vs power, naivety vs wisdom, intuition vs logic, unconscious vs conscious. Which of these interpretations is relevant to you depends on what else happens in the dream and what is currently going on in your life.

Chocolate

Like cakes, confectionery and other types of sweets, to dream of chocolate is a good omen and suggests that you may soon receive a reward, a present or a prize.

Choking

A variation of the drowning or suffocating theme, to dream that you're choking may symbolize that you're finding it difficult to cope with a certain situation in your waking life. Because choking involves difficulty in swallowing, it may be that you're having to 'swallow your pride' in real life. If you're choking someone else in your dream, you may need to ask yourself who is irritating you so much that you want to throttle him/her.

Christmas

Dreaming of a Christmas scene with presents and tinsel and the table groaning with turkey and pudding, suggests the excitement of anticipation. You're expecting to have fun and good things to happen.

Church

To visit a place of worship such as a church, temple or

mosque in your dream may be telling you that you need to take a more spiritual approach to life, or that you're in need of comfort or support. Alternatively, because a church is essentially a building and buildings in dreams symbolize your body, dreaming about a church may be reminding you that your body is sacred and precious and that it shouldn't be abused.

Circus

To dream of a circus suggests that you are looking forward to colourful and exciting events.

Classroom

Since young people spend a lot of their waking time at school, it's not surprising to find that classrooms feature quite often in their dreams. On a basic level, dreaming of something that happened in class may simply be a replay of an event that recently took place at school. Even so, your dream may give the event a particular slant. For example, anything written on the blackboard may be a message. Or a friend may be wearing a bright red sweater which suggests that he or she is emotionally aroused, either angry or passionately in love, depending on the context of the dream. A classroom is also a place of education, so perhaps this dream is telling you there is something you have to discover or to learn. If you're the teacher, perhaps you feel you know something that you have to tell or teach to someone else. In dream lore, rooms symbolize parts of ourselves and whatever is going on in that room describes what is happening to us or how we feel. So, if you dream that the pupils in the classroom are attentive and calm, it suggests that your life is happy and well-balanced at

present. But if the pupils are loud and unruly, it's possible
that you're going through a bit of a hard time.

Cleaning

Symbolically, cleaning is associated with getting rid of
something. If you're cleaning out a messy room, it
represents that you want to 'clean up your act', to shed
something that's on your mind or to get rid of someone
who's hassling you. Perhaps, if you've taken on too many
commitments or you're overburdened with school work,
this dream is telling you it's time to sort out your priorities.
If you're frantically cleaning or washing yourself, though,
it could mean you've got a guilty conscience.

Climbing

Whether you're going up a ladder, making your way up a
flight of stairs, or scaling a mountain, climbing in a dream
symbolizes your need to succeed and conquer. This is
essentially a dream about ambition. An easy climb up a
wide, carpeted staircase means that you will achieve what
you want without any hassle. The harder the climb, the more
difficult you feel it will be to achieve your goal in life,
especially if there are obstacles like huge boulders in your
path, or if the stairs are rickety or dangerous. If you reach
the top, you know you have the power to achieve your goal.
Descending or climbing downwards, especially if you trip
or stumble, may be warning you of problems or setbacks to
come. If you're climbing down the stairs to the basement or
to a dungeon, it suggests that you're trying to explore some
hidden worries or that you want to confront your fears.

Ben's dream

We were going to a talk or a lecture, or something like that, **at the town hall** *and there was a big crowd of us. I remember we had to* **climb up a huge set of stairs** *to the front entrance. The stairs were* **steep** *and all I could see were the legs of the people in front of me climbing up one step after another. It was like* **there were hundreds of legs** *and they were all wearing* **white trousers with dark blue jackets** *above. Someone behind me was trying to push in front of me and that made me cross. I was getting puffed out but I was determined to keep up because I didn't want that pushy person to get past me. When I looked up, suddenly* **all the lights at the windows** *were switched on.*

Interpretation: A dream that involves any sort of climbing is usually making a comment on your ambitions. The harder the climb, the more effort you have to put into your work to achieve your goal. Here, the stairs are steep and Ben is getting puffed out so he is having to work hard. The stairs lead up to a town hall which is a large public building. There's a huge crowd of people climbing the stairs and everyone is dressed in the same clothes which suggests a uniform. All this tends to represent Ben's school, especially so because the crowd is going to a lecture (or lessons, in real life), and the people are all dressed in the same uniform. Ben is in the top stream in all subjects and, because he works hard, he is getting top marks. He admits that he is a competitive person and he likes coming top, so he knows he has to sustain this effort or else someone else will beat him – or, as his dream puts it, push past him. The fact that all the lights are suddenly turned on is a most encouraging sign, and reassures Ben that he will continue to do well.

Clock

Do you have a problem with time? Are you the sort of person who leaves everything to the last minute and then has to rush around frantically to get homework done in time? If so, dreaming of a clock or a watch may be a gentle hint that you should better organize your time. More specifically, the clock may be reminding you that you've made an arrangement to meet someone, or that you've been consistently late for school and you've been threatened with detention unless you show up promptly in the morning. Of course, if your alarm clock actually rings whilst you're fast asleep, your unconscious may weave that into a dream – of a ringing alarm clock!

Clothes

'Clothes maketh the man', so the saying goes, which means that you can tell what people are like by the clothes they wear. In dreams, clothes will say a lot about you personally and about your state of mind. For example, if you're wearing new clothes it suggests you're confident, and if you're buying new clothes it could mean that you want a new image. Ragged clothes, of course, would be the opposite, suggesting a lack of confidence, or a feeling that you don't come up to scratch, or that others judge you as inferior to themselves. Dreaming that you're wearing the wrong clothes for the occasion is an embarrassment dream suggesting that you're afraid of showing yourself up in public. Another classic embarrassment dream is not wearing any clothes at all. Look up **Nudity** to find out the meaning of that dream. Finally, the actual colour of the clothes in a dream can carry a good deal of meaning in itself. If you can recall the colours of your clothes in the dream, look them up under the entry for **Colours**.

Clouds

Just as in real life grey clouds bring rain, so in dreams grey clouds suggest a bad day lies in store. Fluffy white clouds in a sunny, blue sky are associated with happy, carefree times.

Coffin

Dreaming of a coffin, whether you're in it or someone else is, may be frightening but it isn't actually a bad omen. This dream simply means there's a change ahead of you, that you've come to the end of one chapter of your life and a new one is about to begin.

Cold

Dreaming that you're cold may be your unconscious trying to tell you that your duvet has fallen off the bed! Otherwise, to dream of a cold-hearted person, or a cold environment can suggest that you're being a bit stand-offish, or that the person you're dreaming of is mean and cruel, or that you're going through a difficult time in your life.

Colours

We don't always dream in colour and more often than not when we do, we may not even notice. Sometimes, though, one particular colour may hit us with its brilliance. Perhaps we notice that the grass is a stunning emerald green or the sky a wonderful azure blue. Or else we may see a pool of blood: although the blood itself may not be important to the meaning of the dream, its red colour may be significant. In the same way, if you dream of a silver spaceship, it might not be the alien craft that is important but the fact that it is silver. If we notice a particular colour in our dreams, our unconscious mind may be drawing our attention to its symbolic meaning.

Red The colour of passion, red may represent love as well as anger. It denotes energy and vitality and is associated with the heart and the spine. In a dream it might be representing the love you feel for your parents, for a girlfriend or boyfriend or for your best friend. The expression 'a red rag to a bull' reminds us that the colour red may symbolize your anger, hatred and rage. It all depends on how you felt and what else was happening in the dream.

Orange Bright and zingy, the colour orange carries pizazz and attracts people's attention. And that's just what this dream means: you need attention, you want to be friendly, you want to be popular. Orange is also the colour of confidence, so dreaming about it is telling you to hold your head up high and to believe in yourself and value your talents.

Yellow The sun, buttercups, daffodils: all these images may flash the colour yellow at you in your dream. When you dream of a good, strong yellow it's a message about vibrant energy, about cleverness and intuition. Yellow represents your creativity and your artistic talents and it confirms your abilities. It's a sunshine colour that brings light and laughter into your life. So it's great to dream yellow. But, if you see a wishy-washy,

watery yellow, your unconscious may be telling
you that you're low in energy. Perhaps you need
a rest or more vitamins in your diet.

Green   The colour of nature, of plants and of grass, green
is for soothing and healing, and if you've been
unhappy or unwell, seeing the colour green in
your dream tells you you're on the mend. If
you're ill, try this trick: before you fall asleep,
think of the colour green; imagine you're in a
green field with lush green plants all around you;
lie in the green, wrap it around you, fill your
room with it. *Think green...* As you sleep, your
body's natural healing processes will be
energized and help you get better quicker.

Healing isn't the only thing we link to the
colour green, because we also use expressions
like 'green with envy', and 'green as grass'
(meaning naive, innocent, immature). If you are
familiar with these sayings then for you the
colour green in a dream may symbolize those
ideas. Someone flashing green eyes at you in
your dream could be suggesting envy, for
example. Or if, in waking life, you've been
acting in a rather immature way, you may dream
of yourself rolling around on a lawn and getting
covered in grass stains. Here your unconscious is
reminding you of the saying 'green as grass' and
hinting that it's time you grew up!

Blue   The colour of the sky and of water, blue is
associated with communication, with cooperation
and team work. To see a bright clear blue in your
dream is a sign of hope and tells you that things

will probably go just the way you want them to in your life. But of course blue is also linked to moodiness: if you're low, you're said to have the blues. So, to see a dark, sombre blue in your dream may be reflecting a feeling of misery and depression.

Violet

Violet, lavender and purple are known as 'spiritual' colours and when they appear in your dreams it could be your unconscious telling you to become a little more sensitive to other people around you. Or perhaps the opposite applies. Perhaps you're *over*-sensitive, too thin-skinned for your own good. So this dream may be advising you not to always take things so much to heart.

Pink

Pink is a shade of red, but nowhere near as intense. It's a warm colour that reflects harmony and contentment. Pink in a dream tells you that you are growing happier in life. It also means that you're excited about something: perhaps you're waiting for good news.

Black

In dreams, black is considered a negative colour which lowers our spirits down to rock bottom, bringing a sense of gloom and doom. If black is very prominent in your dream, or if you have recurring dreams with a lot of black in them, it suggests that you're going through a sad time in your life when you feel there's no point to anything. But of course a dream can't be all black, otherwise you wouldn't be able to see any of the other images, so it's important to try to remember what other colours you saw. Even a pinprick of light in the blackness would be significant – perhaps the flash of a ruby ring, a corner of a white wall, a darkened tree with a green leaf. Concentrate on the other colours, no matter how small, because this is the way that your unconscious is showing you how you can lift your mood, giving you hope, revealing the way out of your problems.

White Think of white as a clean sheet of paper ready for you to write on. That's one interpretation for a dream where white figures prominently. It means you're ready for something new, you're turning over a new leaf, you're going to start again. To see a shining white light may actually mean that you're about to 'see the light', that you'll find the answer to a problem, understand something that's been puzzling you.

Silver Silver is a precious metal, and dreaming about it is associated with money. Silver is also linked with the moon, with females and femininity. As usual, which interpretation suits depends on whatever else is happening in the dream and in your own life.

Gold To dream of the colour gold suggests that you will have an achievement soon, as this is the colour of success. If you're dressed in gold or are holding something made of gold it's telling you to be proud of yourself because this is the colour that is associated with how much you value yourself and your abilities. Gold is also the colour of coins and is therefore a symbol of riches and wealth.

Computer

This dream may be saying something about your skills. If you're playing a computer game, typing or programming competently, your unconscious is confirming your talents and abilities. If you're making a mess of things on the computer, perhaps you're trying to point out to yourself that you could do better if you tried harder. Take note of what's on the screen, as this in itself may be significant to the meaning of this dream. Alternatively, remember that computers function logically, so that to dream of writing a computer program may be a message that you can solve a problem in your waking life by working at it logically and systematically.

Cooking

Whether it's you or someone else who is doing the cooking, this dream is a good omen foretelling a cosy, contented and comfortable few days ahead. Or are you 'cooking something up', something special, a new scheme or some new ideas?

Corridor

Very importantly, corridors usually link one set of rooms to another, so they are 'in-between' places and that's just what they symbolize in your dream – the fact that you are going through a transitional phase in your life. Also, because corridors are long, narrow passageways, they may represent the journey or the progress you're making in your life. Look up **Alley** to find out the meaning behind this aspect of a corridor in your dream.

Did you know that:
eating cheese before bed really can cause nightmares because a heavy, fatty meal last thing at night can upset your stomach which in turn can give you bad dreams.

Cow

As a docile creature, a cow in your dream may simply represent a peaceful, contented time in your life. Or does the cow have a menacing look about it, and does it remind you of any female you might know? Unfortunately, the word has become a derogatory term that some people use to describe women in an offensive way. If it is a word you use to describe someone you know, that person may well be represented by a cow in your dream.

Crash *(See Aeroplane and Car.)*

Crime

Be careful if, in your dream, you commit a crime, as this may be suggesting that you could be tempted to do something wrong over the next few days in your waking life. If there's someone you recognize in your dream who's committing a crime, it means you suspect that person is dishonest in real life.
(See also Burglary.)

Crocodile

Crocodiles are not good news for dreamers since we associate them with lies and hypocrisy. Think of the 'crocodile tears' which mean pretending to feel sorry, and you get the idea behind this dream. Are you the crocodile who's putting on a pretence or is it someone you know?

Crossroads

Clearly you've reached a crossroads in your life. If there's a signpost, take note of what it says, for here could be a clue to help you make up your mind which way to go. Even if there isn't a signpost, look carefully at the alternative routes in front of you for clues as to which way would be the easiest, or safest, or prettiest, or quickest path to take.

Crowds

Are you being pushed and jostled by the crowd, or are you with a gang of your mates and having fun? If you're being pulled and pushed about in your dream, it may be a message that you're being pushed around by someone, swept along by other people or hustled by a relationship. Ask yourself whether you're being pressurized into doing things you don't really like. If you're having a good time with a group of your mates, this dream is telling you that you feel in tune with friends and relaxed in company.

Crown

To dream of a crown signifies success and rewards coming your way. Your 'crowning glory', no less.

Crying

Dreams of crying mean either that you've been upset in the day and this is a kind of release mechanism for you, or that you may experience a disappointment.

Curtains

When we draw curtains together we are screening or blocking something out. If you dream of this, consider what it is that you're wanting to screen off in your life, or perhaps there is something, a situation or an event that you don't want to confront. Take note of the view that you're blanking out, and of any objects that figure prominently in the room and even of the colours of the curtains themselves. All these can give you clues to whatever problem you're experiencing and point you to a solution. Of course, drawing back the curtains to expose the view or the daylight can mean that you've found an answer to something that's been bugging you. Again, the view that you see from the window can show you what's going to happen next. Another interpretation of this dream is that you're opening a new chapter in your life.

D

Dagger

A dagger is a fascinating but also a complex dream symbol with several different meanings depending on the rest of the action in the dream and on what's going on in your life at the time. Firstly, think of that expression, 'to be stabbed in the back'. Could it be that someone has been bad-mouthing you behind your back? Or perhaps you're being told to watch out because you could be deceived by someone who's being two-faced. So watch your back is the message here. But if it's you who's holding the dagger in your dream, could it be *you* who will be doing the dirty deed in real life to someone you know? If you're attacking someone with the dagger, it means you're angry with that person and are trying to get your own

back. Someone threatening you with a dagger might imply that you're anxious about something. Alternatively, because of its shape, daggers are considered phallic symbols which mean they represent a penis and the dream, therefore, may be expressing something about your sexuality.
*(See also **Running** and **Sex**.)*

Dancing

Dancing in a dream is a sign of joy and happiness. But, if everyone else is dancing and you're just a wallflower on the side it may mean that you're feeling left out in life at the moment.

Death

Nowhere near as dreadful as they sound, dreams about death are some of the most common on record and have been occurring since the dawn of creation. To dream about death or dying, whether it's your own death or someone else's, very rarely has anything to do with an actual death in real life, so don't take this dream literally. What this dream is about is transformation and it means that the dreamer is going through a time of change, a time when one chapter in his/her life is coming to an end and another is about to begin.

Dentist > *(See Teeth.)*

Descending > *(See Climbing.)*

Desert >

To be wandering about in the desert symbolizes loneliness. Perhaps you feel your life is boring and empty and, if so, your unconscious is telling you it's high time you got some new hobbies or made some new friends. On the other hand, if you've eaten something like crisps or salted peanuts before bed you could get thirsty in the middle of the night and then dream that you're lost in the desert and dying of thirst!

Detective

Because detective work is all about following clues and solving mysteries or crimes, to dream about a detective means you will find the answer to something that's been bothering you.

Devil

We've all got good bits and not-so-good bits in our character and we think of the devil as representing those not-so-good aspects about ourselves – our vices and our bad behaviour. If you dream of the devil, it may be your guilty conscience tugging at you for some mischief you may have done. But we also think of a devil as somebody who leads us astray. So, could it be that this dream is warning you about some bad influence in your life, a person or a situation, perhaps, that's leading you to do something you think is wrong?

Diamonds

Sparkling diamonds symbolize truth and beauty, but in dreams this precious jewel can have several different meanings. To be given diamonds foretells that you will come into some money. To lose diamonds, though, suggests you're afraid of losing something precious. A boy/girlfriend maybe? If you're giving a diamond to someone else, your unconscious is telling you to be honest and tell that person the truth. Alternatively, diamonds are cut into facets, so if you dream that you're holding a diamond up to the light and looking at it, your dream is telling you to look at all sides of a situation that's taking place in your waking life. Or else it might be telling you that you should look at all sides of your own character and personality because we are all multifaceted and there's more to each of us than meets the eye.

Diet

There's so much hype about diets these days that it's not surprising to find this subject appearing in our dreams. But dreaming about dieting doesn't only have to do with food: it could imply that you need to cut down on other things, like buying so many clothes, CDs or so much make-up, because you can't afford them just now. So if you do dream that you're going on a diet, before you even start to think that this might be a hint about your body shape, consider whether there are other areas in your life where you're a bit extravagant or frivolous and, if so, whether this is a hint to cut down on those.

Dirt

To dream that you have a dirty face may be suggesting a guilty conscience. Have you done the 'dirty' on someone or do you feel ashamed about a part of your behaviour? Perhaps you need to 'come clean'. If you're wearing dirty clothes in your dream, perhaps it's your image that needs an upgrade.

Disappearances

Quite often, characters in our dreams can vanish before our very eyes. Either one minute we're talking to them and they simply disappear, or else it is the dreamer who appears to be invisible to the other people in his/her dream. Whichever it is, it's the dreamer who is feeling insignificant, worthless, 'invisible' to those around him/her and therefore ignored by them. This dream is hinting that it's time to adopt a higher profile.

Doctor

It would not be unusual to have a dream about a doctor if you'd just been to the clinic, or if you were waiting to go into hospital. In general, though, we think of a doctor as someone who cures our illnesses. Dreaming of a doctor, then, might be suggesting that you're in need of a bit of care and attention. You might have this dream when you've been feeling unwell or you're just going down with a cold. If, however, a doctor in your dream is examining a part of your body, or tells you something about a disease, take note, because this might be a warning to you about your health.

Did you know that:
a dream can last anything from five minutes to half an hour.

Dog

Because a dog is considered to be 'man's best friend', a dog in a dream often represents a mate or companion. If you're playing with a dog, it means you've got a good relationship going with a close friend. Dogs are loyal creatures and fiercely protective of those they love, often intuitively sensing what their masters and mistresses are feeling. So a dog who comes up to you in a dream may be a messenger, bringing you comfort, affection and hope, especially if you've been upset or unhappy recently. But a dog that is vicious or attacks you may represent someone who is being unkind to you.

Doll

Dolls represent people, so a doll in your dream may be standing in for someone you know, especially if it has the same sort of hair or is wearing similar clothes to that person. If it reminds you of a favourite doll that you had when you were little, the dream may be harking back to when you were a small child, so perhaps the message is that you want cuddling and cosseting and need to feel secure.

Donkey

Dreaming of a donkey could be telling you that you're being obstinate and 'stubborn as a mule', or that someone in your waking life is being difficult to deal with.

Door

This is a very important dream symbol. You know the expression 'when one door closes, another one opens': in a dream a door represents an opportunity or an opening – especially if it's standing open in front of you. This dream is telling you to go ahead, to take a chance; it's saying that you're ready and now's the time to make your move. If the door is closed, if you can't, or won't open it, you're probably not quite ready to make any changes in your life just yet and feel you need to wait until the time is right.

Dove

You might dream of this symbol of peace after you've had a row with a friend and want to make it up.

Dragon

Dragons and monsters represent people or situations that frighten you in real life. Colours or other objects in the dream should give you clues to help you pinpoint who, or what, it is that makes you anxious. Turning and confronting or, better still, frightening away a menacing dragon in your dream will give you confidence to sort out the problem in your waking life.

Dream

Some people, while they're asleep, become aware that they are dreaming and, in a sense, they dream-watch themselves having a dream. What happens is that you have a dream inside a dream and you can watch the action of each taking place, rather like watching a play within a play. This 'dreaming that you're dreaming' is known as having a lucid dream. It's quite rare but you can actually learn to do it and when you can, you're able to control the action in your dream and use the information in it to help you in your waking life. For example, if you have a problem, you can make yourself act it through and then go on to find the solution. It's a brilliant technique because it can give you confidence to do something difficult in your waking life.

For example, if somebody is bullying you in real life, you can dream about the sort of situation in which that happens, but then you can direct yourself to confront the bully in the dream, to shout at him/her, or even to chase that person away. This can give you an enormous amount of satisfaction and personal strength and allows you to carry that courage over into your waking life so that next time, you can handle the confrontation with greater confidence. In the same way, if you have a school project to do and you get stuck and can't find an answer, you might be able to 'programme' your dream to give you the information you need. If you want to have a go at lucid dreaming, before you fall asleep simply tell yourself what you want to do, whether it's to sort out a problem, solve a mystery, find an answer to something, or whatever. Keep thinking about this until you drop off. You may need to practise over several nights or even weeks until you can get the technique to work for you.

Drink

If you've had a salty snack before bedtime, you might get thirsty in the night and, if you do, you might dream that you're drinking. That would simply be a way for your body to wake you up so you can get a glass of water. Otherwise, note what sort of a drink you had and whether you liked it or not. A delicious, refreshing drink suggests you'll come up with a new plan or a great idea. A fizzy drink foretells a celebration; a bitter drink is associated with disappointments. Spilling a drink may be a sign that you're wasting your efforts or could be telling you that you're likely to make a mistake or a gaffe of some kind.

Driving

Dreams about driving are symbolically very important. To be in the driver's seat and to be driving along happily means that you're in control of how your life is going at the moment. This can also mean that you feel liberated, or that you want to be free and independent. But if you find there's something wrong with the vehicle, or if you're driving too fast, or going out of control, it means you're not on top of things and you're finding life difficult. Dreaming about driving a car is quite common for a person who is learning to drive in real life and simply reflects the thrills or anxieties that we all feel when we're acquiring this skill. *(See also Car.)*

About sleep
When we're fast asleep we lose muscle tone and our bodies are so relaxed it's almost as if we're paralysed.

Drowning

Drowning and suffocating are different versions of the same type of dream, both symbolizing that you're finding it hard to cope with the demands that life is making on you at present. It could be that events in your waking life are literally dragging you down, or that life itself is a drag. It doesn't have to be water that you're drowning in, and whatever it is that you're sinking into will give you a direct clue as to what is overwhelming you in your life. For example, if you're revising for exams, you might dream that you're drowning in a sea of scrunched up balls of paper. If you shout for help but no one hears your cries, it probably means that you feel there's nobody there to help you sort out your problems in real life.

Drugs

Because taking drugs is a form of escapism, to dream about

drugs may mean that you simply want to escape from a particular situation that you're finding difficult or unpleasant in your life. If you have this dream you should ask yourself what it is that's bothering you or that you're wanting to run away from. Other images in the dream can help to give you a clue or point out a way to solve your problems. Alternatively, this might well be your unconscious warning of the damaging effect drugs can have on your health.

Eagle

An eagle represents power and ambition. Also, because they have such keen eyesight, they symbolize insight. So, if you dream that you're an eagle, soaring high up in the sky, it means you have big plans that you'll probably achieve because you also have vision.

Earrings *(See Jewellery.)*

Eating

Are you eating alone or in company? Do you recognize the location or is it somewhere strange? And what is it that you're eating anyway? All these images will give you a clue to the message that your unconscious is trying to get through to you. Since eating is considered a social activity, if you're dining with a happy crowd, it suggests a happy time lies ahead. But if you're eating alone, you're probably feeling lonely and unloved. To be eating at home, surrounded by your family, is comforting and shows that you're contented with the way things are going in your life. If you're eating in a strange

place, prepare for new adventures. Whether these are likely to be pleasant or otherwise depends on what else was going on in the dream and how you were feeling. Was it a banquet, a cosy dinner for two, or was the food horrid and unfamiliar to you? A lavish feast implies good fortune. A cosy twosome suggests you want to get closer to your boy/girlfriend. But if you're forced to eat food you don't like, it may mean that you're having to put up with a difficult situation.
*(See also **Food**.)*

Eggs

Eggs contain new life, so to dream of an egg in its shell symbolizes a new beginning. For example, you might have this dream when you're getting better after a bout of ill-health. Good health is particularly associated with eating eggs in your dream. Generally, though, eggs in a dream are a sign that opportunities to improve yourself or your life are on the way. Seeing a nest of eggs could imply a 'nest egg', meaning that you could soon receive some money or something valuable. Breaking an egg is associated with making a mistake, whilst rotten eggs imply disappointment.
*(See also **Eating** and **Food**.)*

Elephant

We say that elephants never forget, so to see an elephant in your dream may be telling you that you need to remember something important. If you have this dream, check your birthdays and anniversaries list as soon as you wake up!

Embarrassment

Dreaming about a situation that makes you feel embarrassed

may simply be reflecting something that happened to you in the day that made you cringe. For example, you might have said something totally naff in class and everyone laughed at you, or you might have dropped your dinner down your front just when someone you fancy was walking past. Alternatively, like other dreams where you see yourself naked or sitting on the toilet in a public place, this might be an anxiety dream. The embarrassment in your dream is pointing out a secret worry of being ridiculed in your waking life, being made to feel small and stupid. This, in fact, is a classic dream telling you that you lack confidence in yourself. *(See also **Nudity** and **Toilet**.)*

Embrace *(See Hugging.)*

Emerald

According to ancient dream lore, emeralds stand for good luck and good fortune. However, remembering that emeralds are green and green is the colour of envy, seeing a mate of yours wearing an emerald in your dream may alert you to the fact that your friend is secretly jealous of you. Or perhaps you're secretly envious of her?

Enemy

If you have an enemy in your waking life, then dreaming about him or her is simply a direct reflection of a real life situation which your unconscious is bringing to the fore. Enemies in general symbolize your hidden fears, and other images in the dream should give you clues as to what these are. If you can turn and confront whoever your dream enemy is or, even better, chase him/her away, you will have more confidence when you next have to deal with that

particular worry in your life.
(See Running.)

Escalator

Since escalators can take you up (as well as down), they have the same meaning as both climbing and stairs and so relate to your progress and ambitions in life.
(See Climbing and Ladder.)

Exams

Sitting an exam is a classic anxiety dream which people often have when they have lots of responsibilities and they feel under stress. The worst kind is where you can't answer a single question and that means that in your waking life you're worried about getting something wrong, or that you're afraid of failure in general. Perhaps you feel that you're being tested in some way or by someone in real life. If you dream that you pass your exam with flying colours, it means that you'll cope with whatever you have to do and that you don't need to worry about it.

Exhibition

What's on at the exhibition? Dreams about museums, art galleries or shows where there are things out on display are associated with image – your image in particular – how people see you, how you come across and how you are judged by others. If the exhibits are boring, might it be that you think you need a new look, or perhaps that life is a bit in the doldrums for you at the moment? On the other hand, if what you see is bright and interesting and colourful, then your life is full of excitement and you're feeling pleased with yourself.

Explosion

Sudden explosions are often warnings alerting you to potential trouble ahead. Watch out for arguments with your family or friends, or for problems at school for a couple of days following this dream.

Eyes

Here's an interesting dream which reflects how you're viewing a situation at the moment. If you dream that there's something in your eye, that you need glasses or even that you're going blind, your unconscious is telling you that you're not facing facts or that you're blinding yourself to the truth in your waking life. And if your eyes are closed, you may not be seeing what's really going on around you. Perhaps a friend is trying to hoodwink you or is pulling the wool over your eyes. If you dream of someone watching you or see one single eye, it might mean that you feel you're being watched. Is someone suspicious of you, perhaps, or are you afraid of being found out for something that you've done? Bright, clear eyes show that you've got a clear view and you're understanding what's going on around you. This dream may also be telling you that you have keen intuition.

Face

In a dream, your face is what is known as your 'persona', the character or personality that you present to those around you. To dream about a face, then, may be telling you how other people see you. If you're smiling, you're judged as a happy, easygoing person and, at the same time, this dream implies happiness and good fortune. If you're frowning and miserable, you should consider whether you've been a bit of a wet blanket around your friends lately. This dream may also be a warning of upsets or disappointments to come. If the face in your dreams is dirty, you may be ashamed or feeling guilty about something you've done. If it's covered in zits, you may be secretly worried that others might see the not-so-good side of your character. And if your face appears much larger than it should, your unconscious may be telling you not to become too big-headed!

Falling

This is a common theme that many people dream about and one that often happens just as we fall asleep when our bodies are relaxed and we 'let go'. It's that letting go that makes us associate the feeling with slipping off a cliff or falling into a black pit. Sometimes, though, a dream about falling can actually be a warning of some possible physical danger that could happen, especially if you recognize where you were falling from. For example, if you fell from a balcony on your house it might be that in your waking life you half-spotted that the brickwork of the wall was badly cracked but you didn't exactly take much notice of it. Here, your unconscious is bringing the danger to your full attention. More usually, though, dreams about falling reflect a sense of insecurity, a lack of confidence or a fear of failure in our waking lives. The sort of person who works hard to get top marks in class might have these dreams because he/she secretly fears handing in a bad piece of work and getting told off. Being afraid of failing important exams, for example, or of letting your parents down can trigger these dreams about falling.

Fame

If you dream that you're famous, it means that you're a bit of an attention-seeker. And dreaming that you're surrounded by famous people also means the same thing – that you want to be noticed.

Family

A dream about your family may simply reflect a recent event that took place at your home. Otherwise, a dream about your family, or any family, may be bringing to your attention something about the way you relate to each other. How the people are behaving and what they're saying will give a clue to this dream's meaning for you. In dream lore, though, to see a large, happy family foretells happiness and good fortune coming your way.
*(See also **Brother**, **Father**, **Mother** and **Sister**.)*

Farm

If the farm is tumbledown you can expect to be working hard over the next few days. It might also be warning you that you could lose some money. But if it's a well-kept farm it means you can expect good fortune.

Fashions

Dreaming about fashion and clothes is all wrapped up with the image we have of ourselves and with how we think other people see us. If you dream that you're dressed in

old-fashioned clothes, perhaps you're secretly worried that your friends think you're a nerd. But if what you're wearing in the dream has great street cred and everyone is admiring your clothes, it means you're a confident person, you're well-balanced and you feel you fit in well with your mates. Note what colours you saw in your dream, as these can be very significant.
(See also Colours.)

Father

Seeing your father in a dream may be a direct reflection of your relationship together and how you feel towards him. If he makes you laugh, he could appear in your dream as a clown. If he's the sort who moans a lot, you might conjure him up as a grisly bear. Or you might see him in his working role as a plumber, a train driver, a brain surgeon or whatever. At other times you could simply be carrying over into your sleep an event that occurred during the day. If your dad had bought you a nice present, for example, the happiness you felt at the time may be replayed in your dream. On the other hand, if you had a row, you might dream of him as a double-headed monster. In dream language, though, the father usually represents an authority figure or somebody in a position of power. For instance, he might be standing in for your headmaster, for the local policeman or even for the Prime Minister.

Fear   (See *Nightmare*.)

Feet

Think about the expressions we use concerning feet which might give you a lead to the meaning of this type of dream.

107

To have itchy feet, for example, foretells that you will be travelling soon. To have cold feet in your dream may mean that you won't be going ahead with your plans. But because we need our feet in order to walk, this dream may also be telling you something about your progress through life. For example, if you're dragging your feet, it's saying that you should get a move on, stop wasting time. If you're limping, perhaps you're finding it hard to keep up in class. If you're striding along, it suggests that you're confident about how things are going for you.

*(See also **Shoes** and **Walking**.)*

Fence

Fences are barriers keeping some things in and other things out. What's inside the fence? If it's a beautiful garden, it means everything in your life is rosy and you feel protected against problems or difficulties that might lie outside the fence. If, however, everything is horrible inside the fence, it may be describing difficulties and worries that you're having in life. If so, try to look over the fence or through it – if you see a beautiful view beyond, you know that you can overcome your problems and make your life better. If there's a gate in the fence and you can go through it, you know there's a way out of your difficulties. If you feel trapped inside a fence, you may be feeling frustrated and 'fenced in'.

Did you know that:
everyone dreams even if they swear they don't – it's just that some people can't remember!

Field

What's growing in the field? That's the important clue to understanding this dream. For example, a field full of ripening corn or wheat confirms that something you've been working on will soon pay off and that you'll get satisfaction and praise for your efforts. But a field full of weeds and stinging nettles suggests that you have a lot of talent but you're not putting enough effort into your work. This dream is tugging at your conscience and telling you not to be so lazy. A field that has been ploughed and is ready for planting is saying that the time is right to start something new.

Fighting

If you are in a fight, it means that you are struggling with a problem or have a conflict in your waking life. How the fight ends reveals how you will resolve your problem. If you win, you will find a solution. But if your opponent wins, or you end up bruised and battered, it may be that the conflict is too difficult for you to overcome alone.

Fingers

To see a pointing finger in your dream could be a message. Take note of whatever it is the finger is pointing at, as this will give you the meaning of the dream. Alternatively, this dream may be suggesting that you'll be on the move or going on a journey soon.

Fire

Dreams of fire can be either positive or negative depending

on the rest of the action in the dream. Sitting around a fire is a sign of contentment, feeling cosy, warm, loved and protected. But fire can also symbolize your passions, and if you see a building on fire it could mean that you're either angry or passionately in love. If the fire is out of control, it's possible that you can't handle your feelings because they're so strong. If the fire is put out, or if you dream of a fire engine, it means that you'll be able to get your feelings under control.

Fish

Fish swimming in the sea are a well-known dream symbol representing our undeveloped talents that lie in deep, dark recesses of our unconscious minds. Symbolically, then, to dream of fish suggests that you are becoming more aware of your deeper feelings.

Flowers

Flowers in dreams go with happiness and hope, with good fortune and good times. But if the flowers are dead or dying, it might be a warning that regrets and disappointments are in store.

Flying

To dream that you're soaring high in the sky like a bird is a wishful-thinking dream, symbolizing your ambitions. The higher you fly, the higher you've set your goals. But if, from up high, you can still see the land below, it means you're not getting too carried away because you've still got a firm view of reality. This dream, then, tells you that although you've set your sights high, you do have the ability to achieve your ambitions. But a dream where all you can see is sky and clouds could mean that you're being a bit unrealistic about your capabilities. If you can see yourself flying away, you may be wanting to escape from a problem or a difficult situation in your waking life.

Food

To dream about food may simply mean that you went to bed hungry! Symbolically, though, to dream that you are putting food into your mouth suggests that in real life you need to take someone's advice on board. Bread is a lucky omen, but a wedding cake is said to be unfortunate. Lemons and other bitter foods may mean you don't like yourself at the moment or that you're punishing yourself for having done something wrong. Unpalatable food may mean that you have to make amends, as in the saying, 'to eat humble pie'. Different foodstuffs carry their own symbolic meaning and are listed alphabetically.
*(See also **Eating**.)*

Foreign country

Dreaming that you're in a foreign country where you don't recognize anyone or anything means that you might soon find yourself in an unusual place or a confusing situation. If you try to talk to strangers and they can't understanding what you're saying, it may be that in your waking life you're finding it difficult to make yourself understood.

Forest

Because trees are strong, solid and long-lived, to dream about trees means that you're strong and determined and that you're taking a mature and responsible attitude in your

111

life. But, to see a forest of trees can have either a positive or a negative meaning depending on whatever else is going on in the dream. For example, if you dream that you're lost in a dark, dense forest it means that you're confused and having a few difficulties working things out in your real life. If you're having an adventure in the forest, it shows that life is currently exciting for you. If you're hiding in the forest, what are you hiding from? Perhaps a guilty conscience.

Fountain

Fountains are associated with cleansing and refreshment. To see one in your dream, then, is a sign of renewal, cleaning the old and starting afresh on the new. If you drink from a fountain, it means you'll have an inspired idea. *(See also **Water**.)*

Fox

Since foxes symbolize slyness, dreaming of one could be a warning that someone you know is being a bit sneaky. Or are you the fox in the dream? If you are, ask yourself whether you've been behaving in an underhand manner.

Friend

Dreaming of yourself with a group of friends means you'll soon be having some fun. Your friends don't always appear in your dreams as themselves, but could be represented by other people you know, by your brothers and sisters, perhaps. But you'll know who they're really supposed to be because of similar characteristics or clothes that give you tell-tale clues.

Fruit

We all know that fruit is good for our health, but if you don't eat enough of it, your body may send you a message via a dream showing you a bowl of luscious fruit and implying that you should eat more of it! Sometimes the message of the dream is contained in the symbolism of a colour, so that a red tomato, for example, could represent passion or a green lettuce may suggest naivety and immaturity. Or perhaps it's the shape of the fruit that holds the message, especially in dreams of a sexual nature. Who could fail, for instance, to get the double meaning of a banana?
(See Colour, Food and Sex.)

Funeral

Not as bleak and negative as it first might seem, dreams about funerals hardly ever foretell the death of a person. What they represent, though, is the end of one phase of your life and the beginning of another. You're burying the past in order to make room for the future.

G

Games

Dreams where games are being played tell you something about your skills and abilities in your waking life. Seeing yourself winning at a computer game, for example, shows how quick and clever you are. Of course, if you're losing in the dream, it suggests you'll have to work harder in your waking life to achieve your ambitions. If you're blind-

folded in a game of blind man's buff, you may be blinding
yourself to someone's faults or deceptive behaviour. If
you're on the sidelines watching other people playing
games it's possible you're feeling left out of things. If
you're asked to join in but you refuse, could it be that you
don't want to take part in something that's going on in your
waking life at the moment?

Garden

Because gardens are generally considered to be lovely,
restful places, dreaming of one foretells happiness and
contentment. If you're sitting in one with beautiful flowers
all around you, you probably have a sweet nature and
you're sure to be loved. If the garden is overgrown or has
weeds in it, it may be time for you to take a look at what's
going on in your life and see if things like bad habits or old
behaviour patterns need to be 'weeded out'. A winter scene
with bare trees suggests there's hard work ahead for you –
perhaps revising for a test or clearing out your room. A
dream where the flowers in the garden are wilting or dying
suggests that you're not concentrating on your work
enough and you're letting your talents go to waste.

Ghost

Ghosts and hauntings in our dreams represent everyday
negative forces that we have to encounter in our waking
lives like when someone is unkind to us, for example, or
they may represent people whom we fear. It's how we react
to the ghost that gives the clue to how we will handle those
problems in real life. If in the presence of the ghost we are
calm, our unconscious is reassuring us that we will cope
well with whatever lies ahead. Records show that children

and young people dream about ghosts quite often.

Giraffe

Are you 'sticking your neck out' for someone or for something that's going on in your waking life at present? Or perhaps you're reaching out to someone or reaching for something that you want. Dreaming about a giraffe may symbolize any of these things.

> **About sleep**
> The amount of sleep people need differs from one person to the next. Some people need as much as 10 hours a night whilst others are happy with only 4.

Girlfriend

For a boy to dream about a girlfriend may be wishful thinking if he doesn't have a relationship at the moment. Or, this could actually be a predictive dream telling him that he'll soon meet someone special. Dreaming of hugging or kissing a girlfriend shows an affectionate nature but also tells of a need to be loved. A guy who dreams that his girlfriend is kissing another boy is either madly jealous or suspects his girlfriend is messing him about. Clues about their relationship or about how a girl feels for a guy may be shown by symbols in the dream. For example, if she's looking at a calendar, it may mean she wants to make a date with him. Or, if she's wearing or carrying a mask, it could imply that she's two-faced and deceitful.

Glass

Broken glass in a dream is a warning that you'll be involved in an argument.
(See Spectacles.)

Gold

Gold represents success and to be given a gold medal in a dream suggests that you will achieve something important or else that you will receive a reward. If you are wearing the gold it means you have a good sense of self-worth, that you believe in yourself, so this is a very positive dream. Gold coins are associated with riches, although this can refer as much to your talents or to the things you value in life, like being loved or having a happy home, as much as it does to money and wealth. If you lose gold, you may lose something precious in real life – again, this doesn't just mean money, it could be a friend, or your reputation, or the respect that others have for you. When gold is the predominant colour in your dream look up its meaning under **Colour**.

Grass

Like all dreams which feature plants, the greener and healthier the grass, the better is the omen for happiness and good fortune. Dreaming of luscious green grass carries the message of well-being, that you're growing strong and healthy. Brown, withered grass, though, suggests that your efforts are being wasted. If you're mowing the grass, you should consider what in your life you need to cut out or reduce. That could mean cutting down on the amount of sweets you eat, or not spending so much money on clothes, make-up or CDs, for example. Grass represents green, so read up about that under **Colour** to find out how its meaning might apply to you.

Graveyard

It wouldn't be at all surprising to dream of cemeteries and graveyards if you were watching a horror movie before bed! Dreaming that you're walking through a graveyard on your own may mirror a feeling of loneliness in real life or a yearning for the past. To dream that you're being buried doesn't for one minute mean that you're going to die. Like dreams about drowning, this is telling you that you're under pressure, that your work or your responsibilities are getting on top of you and you're finding it difficult to cope. If someone else is being buried it could mean you want to end a relationship or put a stop to something that is happening in your life. If you're digging a grave, you need to ask yourself whether in your waking life you're 'digging yourself in', that is, behaving defensively, or could you be 'digging your own grave' which means getting yourself into trouble?

Gun

Being shot at could be a warning that you have an enemy. Perhaps someone is saying horrible things to you or about you. Also, because of their shape, guns are considered phallic symbols in dreams, so to dream of a gun may mean that you're feeling sexy.
*(See also **Running** and **Sex**.)*

H

Hair

To dream about long, thick hair is an omen of good health and vitality. Combing through your hair means that you will solve a problem – you'll be teasing out the tangles or the knots in a particular situation. If you're plaiting your hair, you could soon be making a new friend. Washing your hair brings water into your dream, so this is saying something about your emotions. Exactly what this might be referring to will be revealed by other images or actions in your dream. Cutting your hair or visiting a hairdresser suggests you want to make some changes in your waking life: perhaps you feel it's time for a new image. Dirty, unkempt hair, or hair that is falling out means that you're lacking in self-esteem at the moment.

Hands

Think of some of the expressions we use concerning hands, like 'washing your hands of the whole affair'. So, if you dream that you're washing your hands, it might mean that you don't want to have anything more to do with a certain situation in your waking life. To 'dirty your hands' means to get involved in something shady. If you dream that your hands are dirty, you may be suffering from a guilty conscience. If you can't grasp something in your dream it may mean you're having trouble understanding something or someone in real life. And if you can't handle an object, it's telling you that there's something going on that you're finding 'hard to handle' in real life. Threats, anger and aggression are all associated with a fist, so you'll know what this means if you ever dream about fists or punches.

But who's making the fist? You at someone else, or another person at you?

Did you know that:
you're more likely to remember what you've been dreaming about if you wake up immediately after you've had the dream. The longer you sleep on after your dream, the less chance there will be of your recalling it.

Hat

Hats have something to do with status and are a symbol of how important we feel we are in our lives. Prepare to receive a reward, good marks or praise if you dream that you're putting on a new hat. But if your hat is broken or shabby, or if you lose it, you may be about to say or do something that will make you look silly. If someone steals your hat, be careful in your waking life, because that person might be trying to take your place.

Headmaster/mistress

In general, headmasters or headmistresses represent authority figures. But, because these are teachers and it's their job to instruct us, head teachers in a dream can stand in for our consciences, guiding us and pointing out right from wrong. Sometimes our parents can be confused with headmasters/mistresses and vice versa.
*(See also **Classroom**.)*

Dreams

Heart

Whether in poems, in stories, in films or in our dreams, a heart is the symbol of love. To dream of a broken heart means that you're afraid of being let down, hurt, or 'broken-hearted'.

Hen

As possessive creatures always fussing over their chicks, clucking hens in a dream may be suggesting that you're a bit of a fusspot. Or perhaps because hens are a bit domineering, too, your dream is telling you that you're rather bossy. To dream of a white hen means success. A black hen, though, is linked to bad news.
(See also Chicken.)

Hill

Are you having difficulty getting to the top of the hill in your dream? If so, it's possible that you're finding life a bit of an 'uphill struggle'. If you dream of being on top of the hill and looking out over a beautiful view, it means you're feeling great. But if you're up a hill and looking down on a person below, you should ask yourself whether in your waking life you're being a bit snooty and looking down your nose on someone you know. If you're on a hill and afraid that you might slip down, it means that you're worried about making mistakes or that you might show yourself up in some way.

Horse

There are so many expressions about horses and riding that to dream of this animal can have many interpretations and you'll have to judge its meaning by whatever else is happening in your dream. To 'look a gift horse in the mouth', for example, means that you've been ungrateful. Maybe you've been cheated if you're 'taken for a ride'. If you're riding on a very big horse and looking down on someone below, your dream is showing you on your 'high horse' and may be telling you that you've been arrogant or snobbish. But because horses are also a form of transport, riding one in your dream can be representing the progress of your life. If you're enjoying the ride, it means life is OK at the moment. But if your horse rears or bucks, there could be problems ahead. A runaway horse, or one that is difficult to control, suggests that you haven't got to grips with a subject or that you're having difficulty mastering a situation. Sometimes horses can represent your emotions, so that a galloping horse symbolizes that your feelings are racing along. And riding on a horse can also suggest the act of having sex.

Hospital

Because hospitals are places of healing, to dream of one may be telling you that you need a little bit of rest and tender loving care, especially if you've been feeling down or ill recently.

House

To dream about a house is to dream about yourself and your own body. Think of the roof as your head or your mind so that the attic represents your ideas, your hopes and ambitions. The cellar is your unconscious, the dark, hidden part of your personality where your anxieties, fears and undeveloped talents dwell. If the house in your dream is clean as a new pin, then you are on top of things. If the

121

house is messy and cluttered, it's a sign that you may be confused and muddled about something. Being in a strange house might mean that you don't understand something about yourself. An empty room suggests an empty space in your life, that you need to find something to fill your time, or to capture your interest. Rooms that are locked or hidden represent aspects of your own personality that you either haven't as yet developed or that you are keeping secret. If you manage to unlock the door and go through into the room, it implies a breakthrough or that you have found a way to develop your potential in new directions or by changing your attitude in some way. If the outside of the house looks run down, it could be a hint that it's time for you to spruce up your appearance or your image. Another hint that it's time to turn over a new leaf comes from a dream in which a house is up for sale.

Sarah's dream

A group of friends stayed at my **house** *for the night.* **Everyone was asleep** *except for me and my* **boyfriend.** *I couldn't get into* **my room as it was too messy,** *so me and my boyfriend had to share with my mum and dad in their bedroom. We told them me and my boyfriend were just friends. We talked for a short while and then* **I turned out the light.**

Interpretation: Everyone being asleep except for Sarah and her boyfriend suggests that the only two people who matter to Sarah at this moment in her life are herself and her partner. Obviously, then, she is focusing all of her attention in this dream on her relationship. Messy, cluttered rooms in our dreams are symbolic of our own confused thinking, so Sarah's unconscious mind is telling her that she is not thinking clearly about this relationship. Perhaps, in her waking life, she is having some secret doubts about this boyfriend, perhaps she's not sure whether she really wants to go on seeing him or not. Her dream takes her into her parents' bedroom in order that she might compare her relationship with that of her mother and father's. In real life, her parents are happy together and she needs to ask herself whether she is as happy with this boyfriend as they are with each other. The fact that she and her boyfriend talk together for a *short* while is describing the duration of the relationship – either that it hasn't been going for long, or, that it hasn't much longer to go. It is significant that Sarah turns out the light, in effect blacking everything out. The dream, then, is bringing to Sarah's attention the misgivings she is having in waking life about this relationship. At the time of the dream she was beginning to realize that she didn't want to continue with this boyfriend and in fact she ended the relationship (put out the light) a couple of weeks later.

Hugging

To dream that someone hugs you is a sign that you are loved and protected. Having someone's arms wrapped around you in a big bear hug gives you a feeling of security and it's a way for your unconscious to reassure you that you do have the ability and the strength to achieve your goals. If you're hugging someone else it shows you're an affectionate and supportive person. If you're hugging someone who, in waking life, you don't like, it could suggest that deep down inside you really do want to make friends. Or else, this could be a way for your unconscious to tell you that that person is really very nice and if you give him/her a chance, you might find that you could have a good relationship together.

Hunger

If you went to bed without any supper, you may well dream that you're hungry in the middle of the night. Otherwise, we say that we 'hunger' for something when we feel that something is lacking in our lives or when we desperately long for something. Take note of all the other images in your dream as these will point out what it is that you think you're missing out on in your waking life.

I

Ice-cream

To dream that you're enjoying an ice-cream is an excellent omen suggesting that you're feeling quite contented and self-satisfied. On the other hand, is the coldness of ice-cream telling you that you're a cool person, or even pointing to cold emotions – yours or someone else's in the dream? Whichever applies depends on the rest of the action in the dream and what emotions you felt throughout.

Illness

It's not unusual to dream about falling ill if you've been a bit off-colour in real life, as this is a way for your unconscious to tell you that you need to rest or that you should see the doctor. The sort of illness that you have in the dream may match the illness you have in your waking life, so take note of the part of your body that was affected. If you're quite healthy and still dream of becoming ill, it might be a warning that your plans won't work out as you had hoped they would. If for some reason you're worried about someone you know, you might dream about that person being ill.

Insects

In general, dreaming about irritating insects means that you're being annoyed by petty things in your life. If you succeed in swatting them, it means that you will overcome whatever it is that's getting on your nerves. If you can identify the insects in your dream as ants, bees, butterflies, etc., look them up under their individual alphabetical listing. *(See also **Bugs**.)*

Invisibility   *(See Disappearances.)*

Island

A good omen if you're the sort of person who thinks that life on a desert island is an exciting adventure. If you are, then this dream means that happy things are on the horizon for you. But, if for you a stay on a desert island sounds like a life sentence in solitary confinement, then this type of dream is reflecting your feelings of loneliness.

J

Jewellery

Dreaming about jewellery is a type of wish-fulfilment dream. Bright, shiny gems signify your ambitions. To lose or break your jewellery warns of problems ahead, whilst dirty or tarnished jewellery may mean quarrels and disappointment lie ahead. If you find an item of jewellery, though, it could mean you're in for a spot of good luck.

Rings	Eternal symbols of partnerships, rings, particularly gold ones, are associated with happy relationships. But if the rings are tarnished or damaged, it could imply that something is going wrong between you and your partner, as could losing a ring, or seeing a wedding ring on the wrong finger.
Earrings	Because earrings draw your attention to the ear, this dream may be telling you to listen more carefully to what you're being told, or that you may soon be getting some good news.
Bracelet	This symbolises a relationship: whether it's going well or not, and whether it's a good or bad influence on you, depends on whether the bracelet is shiny or dirty, and what it's made of. The more gorgeous or expensive the better. One that's made of rusty base metal (think of manacles!) might not be such a good omen for the success of that relationship.
Necklace	Especially if given as a present, a necklace symbolizes happiness.
Diamonds	As they are symbols of victory, dreaming of diamonds means you will win.
Emerald	These stones are said to symbolize good luck. However, if it's the colour green that's the most significant thing in the dream, then the message has something to do with envy.

Rubies	Rubies may simply represent the colour red, in which case the dream is all about passion.
Pearls	Pearls are like teardrops and are therefore associated with sadness.

Journey

Journeys and travel carry important messages in dreams. That's because whether you're walking, cycling, riding a horse or driving a car, a dream in which you're moving along a road represents your progress in life. Setting off on a journey marks a turning point, the start of a new adventure. You might have this sort of dream before you move house or when you change schools or, of course, just before you set off on holiday. If you're enjoying the scenery in your dream, you're happy with the progress you're making in your life, but you aren't so happy if the environment through which you're travelling is bleak and horrid. What are the colours in this dream? Might there be a ray of sunshine in the distance offering hope and better times ahead? Or can you look down a side street, perhaps, and see a nice garden? If so, there may be a way out of your difficulties, especially if you can turn into the street.

Judge

You may well dream of a judge when you've done something wrong and your conscience is pricking you. Alternatively, judges and law courts may figure strongly in your dreams if, in your waking life, you've been in a situation where you have been misjudged or wrongly accused of doing something you know you didn't do. At other times, seeing a judge in your dreams may be warning you not to prejudge someone or hastily jump to conclusions.

Juggler

A dream about a juggler is saying that you're a busy person, involved in lots of different activities. If the juggler is good, then you're able to handle all the things you've taken on, but if the juggler keeps dropping his/her clubs, perhaps it's telling you that you're involved in too many different activities, or that you're stringing too many boy/girlfriends along at the same time. If that's the case and your school work is suffering, perhaps it's time you cut down on some of those extra-curricular activities that are taking up so much of your time and energy.

Junk shop

To dream of a shop full of junk may be a gentle hint that your room needs a good old clear-out! In general, though, piles of junk suggest that you're bogged down with stuff. This could mean that you have a lot of responsibilities or problems that need sorting out, or that your mind is cluttered up with too many trivial things, or even that you've collected too many of the wrong sort of friends. All this 'junk' is holding you back and the message here is that you need to off-load some of it to clear the way for the next phase in your life. So consider who or what is no longer important to you or to your development and simply junk it/him/her.

Kettle

We associate kettles with cosy things like warm kitchens, tea time, hot cups of coffee – that sort of thing. So if you dream of a kettle boiling on the hob, it gives you a feeling of cosiness, or reassurance, of warmth and nourishment. This suggests that you're happy at home with your family. A kettle that is boiling violently on the stove may mean you're steaming mad or boiling with anger. But if the kettle is cold and the room is bleak, you're probably feeling lonely and unloved.

Key

This is a very important dream symbol, because a key in our dreams, just as in our waking lives, represents finding a solution to a problem. But losing a key implies that a situation will become more complicated and the solution further away. If someone gives you a key, it means that another person will help you find the answer to something that has been bugging you. If you turn a key in a lock, it could be the start of a whole new chapter in your life.

Killing

To dream about killing someone or something is by no means bad and you shouldn't feel guilty or ashamed if you're the one who's doing the bumping off. This is simply another variation on the death dream and it represents the ending of one phase of your life and the beginning of something new. If you're the killer, you're probably discharging your anger about something that's happened in the day. Or else your unconscious is telling you that it's time to finish a relationship or to put a stop to something that you're doing. If you're the one who's being killed, this means you're the victim both in your dream and in real life. Perhaps you're being put upon or taken advantage of. If so, a good way for you to boost your own courage is to force yourself to fight back in the dream and to beat your opponent. If you succeed in the dream, you'll find it easier to stand up for yourself in your waking life.

King

People often dream about kings, queens, members of the royal family or other important celebrities, but the essential thing is how you figure in these dreams. If you are the royal person and are acting condescendingly, your unconscious may be telling you that you're becoming a little too big for your boots! But if a member of the royal family snubs you or belittles you in any way, your dream is suggesting that you have a low self-image and that you need to believe in your talents and assert yourself a little more. Sometimes, dreaming about royalty indicates a desire to be noticed.

Kissing

Who's doing the kissing? – that's the question. Kissing your mum or dad or any other relative you like means you're going through a contented time in your life. Giving kisses to a baby suggests that whatever you're working on will turn out all right or that your problems will soon be sorted out. If you're kissing your girl/boyfriend it means you're happy and comfortable together. But if your boy/girlfriend is kissing someone else, you may be jealous, or insecure about your relationship. Dreaming that you're kissing someone you dislike warns that you may be asked to do a job you hate, like cleaning your room, perhaps, or staying in to baby-sit your little brother.

Did you know that:
you dream on and off throughout the night but you're more likely to remember the dreams you have at dawn rather than the ones you had soon after you went to bed.

Kitchen >

A house in a dream is said to symbolize yourself and your personality and each room represents a different aspect of your personal life. Kitchens are considered the centre of the home, so dreaming about a kitchen is telling you something about what is going on in your family at the moment. If in your dream the kitchen is cluttered and full of rubbish, it could mean that you're finding things a bit complicated and difficult at home. Perhaps there have been some misunderstandings, or you may have had a row with your parents. This dream, then, would be telling you that it's time for you to thrash things out and clear the air. Dreaming of a warm, cosy kitchen where the family is eating, tells you that all is well and that you're happy and contented. If you're cooking in the kitchen it means you're developing a good scheme or idea – you're 'cooking up' something interesting.

Knee >

Dreaming about a part of your body can either refer to the state of your health or it may symbolically represent something that is happening in your life. If your knee figures strongly in a dream, then it might be because you hurt it or cut it during the day. Or it might be warning you of a risk of injuring that part of your anatomy, so watch out over the next few days. Symbolically, because we kneel or curtsy with our knees in an act of respect to somebody superior to ourselves, dreaming about your knee may be telling you to be more respectful to those around you.

Knife > *(See Dagger and Sex.)*

Ladder >

Here is a very important symbol: dreams about ladders are connected with your hopes and ambitions for the future. Climbing a ladder in your dream is similar in meaning to climbing stairs and tells that you're striving to achieve something in your life. If you're enjoying the climb, it means you're confident, but if you're afraid of falling, it's suggesting you lack self-confidence and you're worried about making a fool of yourself. If the ladder has broken rungs, it means there are likely to be obstacles in your way.

Lamb >

To dream of lambs frolicking in a field is a positive symbol which represents a happy family and a cosy home. A lamb that has been separated from the rest of the flock and who can't find her way back, may be a message that you have somehow 'lost your way' or that you're confused or perplexed about a situation in your waking life. If you're the lamb in the dream and you're chasing after the rest of

132

the flock, you should ask yourself whether you're easily led and simply copying everything that everyone else does instead of being true to yourself.

Lamp *(See Light.)*

Leg

You may dream about your leg if you've hurt it or injured it in the day. Alternatively, think of some of the expressions we use with the word 'leg' in them and this will give you a clue to the message in your dream. For example, if you've been arguing the toss with someone even though you know you were wrong, then this dream may be telling you that you 'haven't got a leg to stand on'. If you've done a lot of sport and you're tired out, you might dream that you're 'on your last legs'. If you've slept through the alarm and you're in danger of being late for school, your unconscious may try to rouse you by sending you a dream about your legs as if to say it's time to 'leg it'. A dream where your legs feel heavy as lead so that you can barely walk is telling you that there's a difficult situation in store for you in your waking life that you don't want to confront. Either that, or the dog has fallen asleep on you again!

About sleep

We need less sleep as we get older. Newborn babies sleep most of the day and night. Young children need between 10 to 12 hours of sleep per night whilst their parents can get by with only 7 or 8. Elderly people need even less.

Letter

A fascinating dream because it can sometimes foretell that you will be receiving some news. But the letter itself might contain a message for you, so if you get a chance to read it, do take note of what it says. If you're the one who's writing the letter in your dream, what are you writing about and to whom? This dream means you're trying to communicate something to someone – a secret message to a boy/girlfriend perhaps?

Light

Light of any sort is always a very important dream symbol because it is a sign of hope, especially if you've been unhappy recently in your waking life. If you're in a tunnel and you see a light at the end of it, you can be sure that better times are ahead. If you open a door (and better still go through it) into a scene that's full of light, it means that you're about to start a new, and much better, chapter in your life. If you light a lamp or turn on a light, you will soon find the answer to something that's been puzzling you. A light that's dim is telling you the time isn't yet right for you to act, or perhaps it's saying you need to put a bit more effort into your work if you want to be successful. A lamp that isn't lit in your dream, or a light that goes out, is a warning sign of problems ahead.

Lion

Lions represent power and strength. If you are chased by a lion, it probably represents someone you're afraid of – an enemy, perhaps, who is bigger and stronger than you. If you are stroking or playing with the lion, it means that you can overcome your fears in your waking life.

Lock

This is a fascinating and important dream with all sorts of meanings behind it. For a start, a box or a door that is locked suggests something is hidden from you. Is there anything currently perplexing you in your life? Whatever it is, the answer is in that box or behind that door. If, in your dream, you have a key and you are able to turn it in the lock, it means that you will find the answer to what you're looking for, or that your problem will soon be resolved. If you have the key but you can't, or won't, open the lock, it suggests you're afraid to confront a problem, or that you don't want to know the truth.

M

Make-up

Giving yourself a make-over in your dream means you want a change of image. Perhaps you're feeling uncool in your life, or your clothes or hairstyle may need a bit of updating. If so, this dream is confirming your desire to make yourself look more attractive – particularly to the opposite sex. Because putting on make-up is like putting on a new face, this dream might alternatively be suggesting that you've been two-faced. If you have, then it's your guilty conscience that has triggered this dream. Lipstick in a dream, however, has a sexual link because it emphasises the lips, which dream psychologists tell us represent the external female sexual organs.

Map

Dreaming about a map may be predicting that you will soon be going on a journey. If in your dream you can't make head nor tail of the markings in your map, it's a sign that you're feeling confused and unsure about something in your waking life.

Marriage

Who's getting married and to whom? A dream of wishful thinking may be one in which you get hitched to your favourite rock singer or film star. If you dream that your boyfriend is marrying someone else, is he really two-timing you?

Mask

Masks in dreams warn of deceit. If you're wearing the mask in your dream, you need to ask yourself if you've been devious or two-faced. If someone else is wearing a mask, your dream is arousing your suspicions that that person is not all he or she pretends to be. Perhaps in your waking life you have half-noticed inconsistencies in that person's behaviour or in what he/she says. Now, your unconscious is bringing those misgivings to your full attention so that you can be more alert and look into those suspicions when you wake up.

Medicine

If you're taking medicine, or someone else is dishing it out to you, it could mean that you are being paid back for something you did, as in the expression, 'having a dose of your own medicine'. If you're giving the medicine to someone else, perhaps it's you that's getting your own back?

Did you know that:
children dream more about animals than adults do.

Mole

To dream of a mole burrowing underground suggests that you need to do some 'digging around' in your waking life. Perhaps there's a mystery you need to uncover, perhaps you don't know all the facts in a situation, or perhaps someone is trying to keep you in the dark for some reason. One way or another, there's more to the situation than meets the eye and if you want to find out what it is, you'll have to root around a bit in order to find out the whole truth.

Money

In a dream about money, a lot depends on who's got the dosh and what that person is doing with it. For example, if someone gives you money, it's a great omen which promises that you'll receive something to your advantage in the near future: not cash necessarily, but something that you'll consider important or valuable nevertheless – maybe a present or a compliment that will make you feel good about yourself. Finding money could imply that you will learn something new or that you will gain self-esteem in some way. Or maybe you will soon meet a lad/girl who's very generous and has a heart of gold. Losing money tells that you lack self-confidence.

Dreams

Moon

The moon and romance go together like a stamp and a letter. To see the moon in a cloudless, star-lit sky bodes well for you and your boy/girlfriend, because it means you're happy together. But if you see clouds crossing the face of the moon, or the moon being darkened by an eclipse, it may be warning you of problems looming on the horizon. The moon is a symbol of peace, so if you dream of a full moon, it means that you're relaxed and contented with the way things are going. Yet another meaning attached to the moon is that she represents creativity. So, to dream of a crescent moon may be encouraging you to develop a sensitive, creative or artistic talent. Finally, dream researchers have discovered that as the moon is linked to the female menstrual cycle, some women dream of the moon just before their monthly periods are due. Here is the unconscious at its most practical, giving the dreamer a useful and timely reminder!

Mother

To interpret this dream correctly very much depends on how you get on with your mother. If she's the sort who always backs you up and you get on well together, seeing her in your dream will reflect that you feel happy and looked after. But if you and your mum argue and fall out all the time, your dream may be referring to a quarrel you've had or warning you about a possible disagreement with someone else, perhaps a teacher. In dream lore, however, mothers stand for protection and nurturing. They represent females in general. Sometimes they symbolize nature or Mother Earth and, if elderly, may represent wisdom, giving you guidance and good advice.

Mouse

Do you behave like a little mouse – quiet, anxious, some-what insignificant? Dreaming about a mouse may be a subtle hint from your unconscious telling you it's high time to break out and project yourself more. If, in the dream, you're a mouse and you're being chased by a cat, it suggests you're afraid of someone or something. What or who does that cat represent? Can you, in the dream, turn the tables on him like Jerry does in the cartoons with Tom? If you can, it means you'll have the strength and courage to confront your fears in your waking life.

Mouth

Full, luscious lips have a sensual meaning, so if you dream about them perhaps it's because you're feeling sexy, or are trying to attract a special person to you in your waking life. Thin lips, though, are associated with meanness, so to dream about these warns that someone may be bitchy to you in the next couple of days. If the lips are moving, or saying something to you, pay attention, because this could be a way for your unconscious to give you an important message. Alternatively, if it's your mouth and you tend to be on the talkative side, could it be a reflection of you as a bit of a motormouth? Or might it be that you've been mouthing off at someone lately? Only you can tell.

Music

To hear music in your dreams means that you are untroubled or at peace with yourself. Music in a dream is often associated with happy times. Famous musicians like Tartini, Stravinsky and Paul McCartney have told how some of their best tunes or compositions came to them in a dream. So, if you dream of a catchy number, hum it into a tape recorder as soon as you can – it might make you a fortune one day.

Necklace *(See Jewellery.)*

Needle

Needles are used for mending and for stitching things together so, if you've fallen out with a mate, this dream may be telling you it's time to patch things up, to make amends. Threading a needle suggests you will successfully find a way to accomplish your aims, but failure to thread a needle could imply that your plans won't work out at all.

Newspaper

Catch the headlines if you can, because they might contain an important message for you.

Nightmare

Nightmares, dreams that are filled with fear and terror, can be very disturbing and can upset us for days after having had them. Some even recur, coming back time after time and repeating the frightening actions and images in exactly the same way. But awful as they might be, nightmares can be very useful because they bring to our attention our innermost secret anxieties. They also help us to release our fear, otherwise all that emotion would get locked up inside us and possibly come out in our waking lives in some other damaging way. When you have a nightmare, it's important that you try to work out who or what terrified you. If it's a monster, for example, you need to ask yourself what it looked like, or who it reminded you of. There will be clues in your dream, either a feeling or a physical characteristic that will help you identify who or what the monster was representing. Did you feel lost, abandoned; were you about to fall or crash; was someone trying to suffocate or stab you? Look up these images and feelings separately under their alphabetical listing to give you the meaning behind this sort of dream. If you do have a frightening dream, a good trick is to force yourself to go back into that dream and confront whatever it is that's threatening you. Or else think it through carefully when you wake up, but give it a new ending, one in which you win in the end. Facing the fear in your dream and chasing it away will give you the strength and confidence to face that fear in your real life.

Did you know that:
girls dream more about houses and relationships while boys tend to dream about machinery and sport.

Nose

Whenever a part of your anatomy is featured in a dream, your unconscious may simply be trying to tell you that there's something wrong in that area of your body. Here, perhaps a recent bruise or injury to your nose is being replayed in your dream. If you dream that your nose is cold and red, you may be starting a cold. A blocked or stuffed-up nose, though, may be forewarning you of a problem to come, because blockages in our dreams symbolize hurdles or difficulties in our waking lives. Another warning of problems is a dream about a broken nose – again, breakages mean a rough ride ahead. Think also of the sayings involving noses. 'Cutting off your nose to spite your face', for instance, may be conjured up in your dream if you've been nasty and tried to do the dirty on someone and it backfired on you. And, of course, a dream where people are pointing to your nose may well be a gentle hint that you tend to be a bit of a Nosey Parker!

Nudity

A classic dream that most people have at some time or other. There are lots of variations of this type of dream but essentially it's about the dreamer being naked in public. For instance, you might be walking into school and discover that you haven't got any clothes on, or you might be shopping in the middle of Tesco's and wonder why everyone is staring at you and when you look down you find you're completely starkers. How you feel about being naked in the dream is the key. Mostly, dreamers feel horrendously embarrassed and this reflects what's known as a fear of exposure, a fear that, in our waking lives, we will commit some horrible mistake or make a fool of ourselves and everyone will laugh at us. Or perhaps we might fear that people will see through us if perhaps we tell a little white lie, or pretend we know something we don't. Another meaning could be that we're giving away too many secrets about ourselves. If, however, people are admiring the dreamer's naked body, it reveals that that person likes to be noticed.

Numbers

There are stories of people who have dreamt of a string of numbers, used them in the lottery – and won! It would be nice if we could all do that, but, alas, this sort of thing doesn't happen very often. Numbers have been recognized as powerful symbols by civilizations and cultures throughout history. They play a particularly relevant role in mystical and religious traditions. Just think how many references there are to particular numbers in the Bible: one, three and seven especially stand out. Jung, one of the greatest experts on dreams, recognized the significance of numbers in our dreams and made a study of their symbolism. Quite often, though, a dream about numbers can have a much more humdrum explanation. For example, you might have this sort of dream if you were struggling with some maths homework before bed, or if you were playing bingo with the family. If it's your house number, your dream may be telling you something about your home or your family. If it's your own age, then the dream is referring directly to you: perhaps you're worried that others think you're a bit childish, or maybe you've been behaving like an old mother hen recently. If it's your telephone number that you dream about, perhaps you're waiting for news. Or could it be that you're expecting a special some-one to call you?

Numbers, however, have been used symbolically for thousands of years and their meanings and characteristics have been recognized by many learned people. Pythagoras particularly liked the number three and believed it was the perfect number because it describes the fusion of body, mind and soul. The significance of numbers is so funda-mental that their meanings are part and parcel of the collective unconscious, so that even if *you're* not consciously aware of what a number represents, your unconscious *is*! If a particular number stands out in your dream, it could well be worth you considering whether its symbolic meaning applies to you or to what is going on in your life at the moment.

One This may actually refer to yourself, as in the expression 'Number 1' meaning me, I, myself. Are you being selfish, are you putting yourself first? It can also mean achievement and success, as in coming first and winning a race. This dream might be telling you that you have the power to succeed at whatever it is you want to do.

Two Two's a couple, so this number could be referring to you with your best mate or to you and your girl/boyfriend. Two is also the symbol of balance, so here your unconscious may be trying to tell you that you're going a little over the top perhaps, or alternatively that you're under-achieving. Either way, you need to look at your behaviour or at what you're doing and see if you can even things out.

Three This is the number of fun, fun, fun. It symbolizes talent, creativity and self-expression. If the number three figures prominently in your dream, you're being prompted to listen to your intuition or go with your gut feeling in any creative or artistic project you're doing. Three is also linked to communication, so, again, follow your instincts if anyone asks your advice or if you're involved in a discussion of any sort.

Four | Steady, solid hard work is the meaning behind the number four. If this number shows up significantly in your dream, it's possible you're being advised that you need to discipline yourself and organize your work better. Get your shoulder to the wheel if you want success is the message of this dream.

Five | Adventure and the number five go together. To dream of this number suggests that you feel you need to spread your wings and consider your options. You don't want to be tied down, but need to be free to do your own thing. You might have this sort of dream, for example, when a girl/ boyfriend comes on too strong for your liking.

Six | This is the number that symbolizes honesty and reliability. If the number six stands out in your dream, it may be pointing to someone who is genuine and sincere, someone you can trust, and whose advice is worth listening to.

Seven | Seven is a bit of a highbrow number with links to knowledge and inner wisdom. Seven symbolizes poetic thoughts, spiritual or religious ideas, music and painting. If you dream of this number, your unconscious may be suggesting that you should think about things more sensitively. Or, if you're a bit of a dreamer, this is telling you it's time to come down to earth.

Eight | In some countries eight is a lucky number because it symbolizes money. Wealth, riches and success are tied up with the number eight, but these have been gained through hard work. So if you've been working hard and you see an eight in a dream, it might be telling you that you'll get your reward soon. If you've been a bit laid back, this dream is nudging you to pull your finger out!

Nine This number is associated with kindness and generosity, with unselfishness and a desire to help others. If you dream of the number nine, it may mean that you'll soon be doing something nice for someone in need, spending your lunch hour explaining the history assignment to a class mate, or offering to run an errand for an elderly neighbour. Or, if you've been a bit mean and selfish lately, this dream might be ticking you off.

Ten The number of perfection and completion: have you just finished a project you've been working on for a long time? If so, you might dream of the number 10.

Nurse

Nurses and doctors appearing in a dream suggest you need to take care of yourself. For instance, you may dream about a nurse if you've been unwell or if you're in need of a little tender loving care. Alternatively, if you've had a row with your best friend, dreaming that you're a nurse may be a way of telling yourself that you need to 'heal' the rift between you and your mate.

Oar

If you dream that you're rowing a boat with an oar, it means you're feeling in control of what's going on in your life. The opposite to that would be a dream where you lose your oar, or where you dream about a boat without any oars at all. Either of these means that you're feeling confused, adrift, things are a bit out of control, and you can't seem to get a handle on the situation. Other symbols in your dream will tell you how you can resolve these difficulties: for instance, you might find a piece of driftwood that will substitute for a missing oar. If you do have an oar but you're not rowing very hard and you're not getting anywhere, this dream is telling you to put more effort into your work. Rowing round and round in circles means you're stuck in a rut and perhaps it's time you found a new tack or a different direction to bring some interest back into your life.

Old people

An old woman in your dreams symbolizes wisdom. An old man stands for knowledge and experience. If they speak to you, listen to what they say, as it's likely to be good advice.

Oven

If you dream about an oven or a cooker it means you're 'cooking up' an idea, a project or a scheme.

Owl

An owl represents both wisdom and keen insight. Because

an owl is famed for its sharp vision, dreaming of one may be telling you that if you look more clearly at a particular situation you will find the right solution. Perhaps your dream owl will land on the answer for you, so look up the meaning of any other objects or animals that you see in your dream. And listen carefully to anything the owl might say because those will be wise words.

Palace

Buildings usually represent our own selves in our dreams with the attic and roof symbolizing our minds and the cellars standing for those as yet undeveloped talents that we possess. The type of building we dream about gives us an idea of how we think about ourselves, whether we feel strong and proud as a fort, humble and insignificant as a basic shack, or tired and faded as a tumbledown ruin. Naturally, then, the grander the building that we dream about, the more confidence and self-esteem we are likely to feel. Since you can't get very much grander than a palace, this is a healthy dream confirming that you feel good about yourself, that you're the tops.

About sleep

When we sleep, we go through cycles of light sleep followed by deep sleep and then up into light sleep again. This forms a pattern that lasts for about 90 minutes and then repeats itself again and again throughout the night. During an average night we may pass through five or six of these complete cycles of sleep.

Paralysis

This sort of dream may have a simple physical explanation. For example, you might dream that you're paralysed and can't move if you've been lying heavily on your arm in your sleep and it has gone numb. Alternatively, this type of dream may be symbolically telling you that you are powerless to act in a certain situation that's going on in your life. Or it might mean that you're rigid with fear, in which case you need to consider what is causing this anxiety in your life.

Parcel

Receiving parcels and packages is associated with news and surprises. The message of the dream may be symbolized by the contents of the parcel, so look up each item separately. If you're sending a parcel, it means you're getting rid of something, someone or some behaviour you have now outgrown or no longer need. This could mean anything from deciding never to bite your nails any more to finally breaking off with a mate who's not a very good influence on your life. If, in your dream, you're lugging around a heavy parcel, it means you feel weighed down with a problem in your waking life.

Parents

Dreaming of your parents may simply be replaying an event that occurred to them recently or it may be confirming how you feel about them. Alternatively, your mum and dad may represent other people, standing in for your teachers, for example. Dads often represent authority figures in our dreams, whilst mums can symbolize comfort and nurturing.

Park

To dream of a lovely park full of trees and plants and lots of emerald green grass is a very good omen, because it means that everything in your life is OK just now. A green park can also mean hope and the promise of better times to come, especially if you've been having a few problems in your life lately. However, if the trees are barren and the plants in the park are dying, it suggests that your problems have only just begun. A park that is strewn with litter and other rubbish may be telling you that your room needs a good old clear-out.

Parrot

Because parrots are great mimics, if you dream of one you should ask yourself whether you're just repeating what everyone else is saying instead of thinking for yourself. So be yourself and do your own thing.

Party

Much depends here on who's giving the party in this dream and whether people are having brilliant fun or are bored out of their skulls. If you are the host or hostess, the dream could either mean that you're terribly popular or it could mean quite the reverse, that you don't think you are popular in your waking life and you wish you were. If you dream you're at a really groovy party and everyone is happy and there's lots of dancing going on, it suggests that your life is busy and everything is going well for you. Having a miserable time in your dream party reflects that life isn't too hot for you right now.

Path > *(See Journey and Road.)*

Peacock >

Either this dream is hinting that you've been showing off, or it's bringing to your attention someone you know who is being rather vain at present.

Pen >

Dreaming that you're writing with a pen or a pencil means there's something you want to say, something you need to get off your chest. To give yourself a clue try and read whatever it is you're writing.

Did you know that:
young people tend to have more nightmares, recurring and predictive dreams than adults do.

Perfume >

To smell perfume in our dreams is quite rare, but it can happen now and again. A nice fragrance is a good omen and promises happiness and success. A foul pong, as you can imagine, however, doesn't bode well at all.

Pig >

No matter how lovable some people find them, pigs in our dreams do not get a good press. Generally, these creatures represent the coarser side of human nature – greediness, selfishness and bad manners. Someone who 'pigs out' or who is pig ignorant, who is porky or in any way behaves like a pig may well appear in your dream as this farmyard creature. Don't forget, though, that the male pig is called a boar, and a person who is a crashing bore may also be symbolized by a pig in your dream.

Plant

Dream plants represent your life and energy, so the greener and more luscious they are, the healthier and stronger you are. To see lovely plants in your dream also means that you're happy and contented. Plants that are wilting and losing their colour could be telling you that you're flagging a bit and need to rest up. A dead plant means that your plans may go awry. If you're repotting or planting out your plants, you're probably a caring person. If your plants are growing in a row, as in the nursery rhyme *Mary, Mary Quite Contrary*, they may be representing the people that you love. And if in your dream you're watering the plants, it means you want to shower those people with your love and affection.

Post

Expect to receive news or information in the very near future if you dream of a postman or of letters dropping through the letterbox.

Presents

To be given a present in your dream means that someone thinks very highly of you.

Prince and princess

Very young children often dream about princes and princesses, because they figure so prominently in fairy stories and films. But, however old we are, members of the royal family symbolize glamour, a rich and easy lifestyle and few money worries. Honour, power and respect are also qualities that we associate with nobility. For many reasons, then, dreaming about princes and princesses may be considered as wishful-thinking dreams. If you dream that you're a prince/princess, it means you want to better yourself. If you meet or talk to a prince or princess in your dreams, you may soon be meeting some exciting people. And, of course, if you've just fallen in love, your new boy/girlfriend may well appear in your dream as a handsome prince or a beautiful princess.

Prison

Prisons are places of restriction, so to dream that you're in jail means that you're feeling frustrated or isolated in some way. This is the sort of dream you might have if, for example, you've been grounded for breaking the house rules or if you live so far out of town that it's difficult for you to get together with your friends.

Prize

Achievement and prizes go together, so if you dream that you're awarded a prize, you may soon be rewarded for something you have done. Perhaps you'll get a special mention in assembly or a cup for winning a race, or excellent marks in a test.

Purse > *(See Bag.)*

Quarrel >

If you're having a quarrel in your dream, it means that you're either replaying a row that's already taken place or that you are expecting an argument to blow up. Whoever you're quarrelling with in the dream will give you a good clue to who you're going to be falling out with in your waking life. However, dreaming of a row may not always lead to a quarrel in real life, because it might just be describing how you're angry with someone and this is a way for you to harmlessly release all that emotion. Sometimes, if the quarrel isn't angry, but more in the way of a heated discussion, it might symbolize two sides of an argument. This might happen if you have to make an important decision and your unconscious is trying to get you to see both sides of the picture.

Queen >

A dream that you're meeting the Queen is a good omen and means that you will be selected for a special merit. Dreaming that you're part of the Queen's entourage suggests that you need to be noticed. For a woman to dream that *she's* a queen is either wishful thinking or a gentle hint from her unconscious that she's behaving a bit uppity in waking life. Queens and mothers may sometimes be interchangeable in dreams, so your mother may be represented by a queen or a queen may be standing in for your mother.

154

Race

Movement in our dreams, such as running or driving, often describes the sort of progress we are making in our lives, so these types of dreams are extremely important. To dream that you're watching a race may be telling you that life is whizzing by and that you're having to work really hard to keep up with everything that's happening. Or it could be describing a competitive situation you are experiencing, especially if you're running in the race yourself. For example, you might have this dream around exam time because sitting an exam is, after all, a competitive business. Or might there be some jealousy or rivalry between you and your mates? What happens during the race and who wins will give you some clues as to how things are likely to turn out in your waking life.

Rags

Do you think it's time you updated your image and got yourself some new clothes? Dreaming that you're wearing rags may be a subtle hint from your unconscious that you take a hard look at yourself and improve how you come across to others.

Rain

Rain washes clean and freshens the air, so to see rain falling in your dream suggests a washing away of all your fears and uncertainties in readiness for a fresh start. A violent downpour, though, may be warning you of stormy times ahead. You may, however, dream of rain if it is actually raining outside as you sleep: your unconscious is giving you the latest weather forecast!

Rainbow

Just as in the story of Noah and the flood the rainbow marked the drying up of the waters and the promise of new life, so dreaming about a rainbow is a wonderful symbol of hope and success for the future. But colours in dreams are significant and a rainbow may be a way for your unconscious to alert you to the symbolic meaning of a particular colour, especially if one of the colours appeared more vibrant than the rest. To find what that colour represents in a dream, see under **Colours**.

Rat

Rats don't get a good press either in real life or in your dreams. Think of the things we associate with the rat – plague, dirt and disease. A rat is a person who betrays you or who lets you down. And of course someone who 'rats' on you is a snitch, an informer, a grass. So, if you dream about a rat, it could be a warning that someone you trust or rely on will let you down, or that a mate may tell on you or deceive you in some way. A hoard of rats is another negative symbol and represents problems and complications.

Rave *(See Party.)*

Raven

Ravens are usually seen as messengers, often bringing bad news. If this is a warning dream, other images will give you clues about what to watch out for over the next few days in your waking life. Ravens are also associated with the unknown, with those parts of our personalities that we haven't as yet developed or explored. Dreaming of a raven flying high in the sky, for example, may be telling you that you have masses of potential to do very well in a particular subject if you just give yourself a chance.

Ring

If you dream that you're standing inside a ring it means that you are protected and secure.
(See also Jewellery.)

River

Rivers contain water, which in our dreams is linked to our emotions. Is the river flowing smoothly, gently babbling on its way, or is it a torrent filled with huge boulders and dangerous undercurrents that could sweep you away? The first tells you that your emotions are under control, that you're happy and contented in your life. The dangerous river is a warning of a possible upset ahead and suggests that you might end up emotionally out of your depth.
(See also Water.)

Road

A road or street is a very important dream symbol, because to walk, run, cycle or drive down a road, street, path or lane is a comment on the sort of progress you are making in life. If you recognize the place and know where you're going, then things are going well in your everyday life. If the road is unfamiliar, it means that you're going through new experiences. What's the environment like in the dream?

157

Can you see flowers, trees and green fields or are you in a run-down neighbourhood with litter on the pavement? A pleasant environment is reassuring, but horrid surroundings suggest difficulties and disappointment. Is it possible to take a detour in your dream, turn back if you want to, stop and look around, or do you feel you have to keep going on and on and on? A detour suggests that you can change your mind, explore alternative possibilities. Stopping to look at the scenery means you have time to enjoy what you're doing and you are able to consider your options. But being forced to follow the road means that, in your current waking life, you have no other choice but to keep on going as you are.

> **Did you know that:**
> talking in your sleep is very common. It's actually possible to have a conversation with someone who's dreaming without him or her waking up.

Rocks

Rocks and boulders symbolize obstacles in your waking life, problems that you need to sort out or to avoid. A large rock in front of you will either need to be climbed over or walked around, so you may need to make an extra effort (climbing over) or do more work (walking further) in order to make your plans work.

Robin

A robin is a brilliant omen in a dream. It promises luck and love and brings messages with glad tidings. Robins are also associated with new beginnings, so you may dream of one just as you're about to start a new phase in your life.

Robot

If you dream that you're a robot you should ask yourself whether you're behaving rather mechanically, at everyone else's beck and call, doing things without questioning why. If so, perhaps this is your unconscious telling you it's time you started thinking for yourself. Stop being a robot, get real, be yourself. But remember that robots don't have any feelings: so, if you're the robot in this dream, it could mean that you're behaving heartlessly or, if you recognize the robot as someone else you know, is he or she rather callous and unsympathetic?

Roller-coaster

If this dream is interpreted literally, it symbolizes the ups and downs of your life. Looking at it symbolically, you need to ask yourself whether the thought of a ride in a roller-coaster makes you excited or frightened. If it thrills you, then you can expect some excitement to head your way. If it scares the pants off you, perhaps the message is that you have a challenging time ahead.

Roof > *(See House.)*

Room > *(See House.)*

Royalty > *(See King, Queen, Prince, Princess.)*

Rubbish

Seeing rubbish lying around in a dream suggests the litter and clutter of everyday life, the things that we no longer need and we throw away. If you're emptying the bin, it means you're growing out of old habits or behaviour patterns that don't work for you any more, or that are now too childish. This can also apply to friends. Perhaps you're drifting away from mates who bore you and you're about to make exciting new ones. If you look around and you see rubbish everywhere, it means your life is a bit bleak and you're going through a difficult period. But if you see a garden or a park in the distance, if the sky is blue, or if a side road leads to a nicer part of town, it suggests there is a way out of your difficulties and life will be a good deal better soon.

Running

Being chased, running away or escaping from something or someone are common dream themes which mirror a situation that is troubling or worrying you in your life. What or who you are running away from in the dream and how you deal with your pursuer may give you some valuable clues to that problem. For example, someone who is being bullied might dream of being chased by a vicious dog. If the dreamer turns and confronts the dog or, better still, throws stones at it and manages to drive the animal away, the dream is telling the dreamer that he or she has the power to overcome the bully in real life.

Saddle

If you ride, or hang about horses a lot, dreaming about equestrian gear would not be unusual for you. In general, however, if you think of the expression 'to be saddled with', it might give you a clue to what this dream is trying to tell you. Perhaps you feel weighed down by responsibility, lumbered with a problem or tied to a promise you wish you hadn't made.

School

It's not surprising that teachers and pupils often dream about school since they spend a large part of their day there. A dream about a school may just be a straightforward replay of something that happened there recently. But because school is a place of learning, this dream may be trying to teach you something, an important lesson about life, perhaps, or bringing to your attention some information that you might have missed in the day. (For more interpretations of this dream look up **Classroom**.)

Sea

Always remember that water in a dream represents your emotions, so, when you dream about the sea, you are describing your own feelings to yourself. If the sea is calm, you're going through an easy time when you're in control of your emotions. But if the sea is stormy, it suggests that you're emotionally worked up.

Sex

Dreaming about sex can be a way of releasing tensions and emotions and it's not unusual to actually experience an orgasm in your sleep. It's quite common for men to get erections while they sleep and teenage boys do go through a stage in their lives when they have what's known as 'wet dreams', where seminal fluid is released from their penis.

Dreams about love and sex are not only natural and healthy, but they can also be very enjoyable too!

Some dreams about sex are all to do with wishful thinking. For example, if you fancy someone like crazy but, no matter how much you flaunt yourself at them, they still look right through you, you might actually get off with them in your dreams (and it can be brilliant). There can't be a person alive who hasn't at one time or another had sexual fantasies about a pop star or famous actor and dreamt about having sex with them.

But dreams about sex needn't just be connected to getting off with someone. Sometimes they tell us something important about ourselves. For example, if a woman dreams she has a penis, it doesn't necessarily mean she secretly wishes she were a man. It's more likely to mean that she's recognizing her 'masculine' qualities – strength, assertiveness, competitiveness, logical mentality – or whatever characteristics she considers to be masculine. And if a bloke dreams that he has breasts, it doesn't mean he should see a doctor about a sex change but merely that he should recognize his more caring, nurturing and intuitive instincts. Don't forget we all possess a mixture of both masculine and feminine qualities, so these sorts of dreams can make us aware of our basic nature and bring to light some of our hidden talents.

There are many types of dreams about sex and lots of different symbols can represent our sexual organs or the masculine/feminine sides to our personalities. For example, knives, snakes, towers or anything long and slender may symbolize a penis and these are known as phallic symbols. Things like boxes, tunnels, bags, caverns and even ovens can represent the uterus and vagina or what we consider to be the feminine side of our nature. The Victorians, who were very straight-laced, used to be really hung up about dreams involving sex and love-making but nowadays we're much more understanding and we accept that sex is a natural part of our lives. It seems obvious, but researchers have discovered that dreaming about sex becomes more common after puberty as we develop sexual awareness and start to become interested in members of the opposite sex.

Our first sexual experiences will set the tone for the sort of sex dreams that we're likely to have during our teens. For instance, if our first sexual encounters are in any way disturbing or scary, we're more likely to have nightmares about being attacked, or we might dream about houses that are burgled or even that we're wearing dirty clothes. But if our early experiments with sex are gentle and loving, or fun and exciting, our sexual dreams are more likely to contain romantic scenes where our fantasies of getting off with hunky blokes and gorgeous girls are fulfilled.

Did you know that:
it's more common for young children to walk in their sleep than it is for adults or teenagers.

Scissors

Is there anything in your behaviour that you need to 'cut out'? For instance, you may have certain habits (like biting your nails or leaving your dirty clothes all over your bedroom floor), that it's time you now outgrew. Or perhaps you're in with an immature crowd who you know has a bad influence on you, and you know it's time you should 'cut loose' from them. Or if you're in a strange environment, you may be feeling lonely, 'cut off' from the people and places you know and love. Any of these situations may give rise to a dream about a pair of scissors and it will be

the other images and feelings in the dream that will give
you a clue to its meaning.

Sheep

If you're watching a flock of sheep peacefully grazing in a
field, it means that you're contented and things are going
well for you. But if you're one of the sheep tagging along
with the rest, your unconscious may be telling you you're a
bit of a 'yes' man or woman and it's time for you to stop
mindlessly going along with the crowd but to stand up for
yourself. The message here is plain: be more individualistic
and be yourself.

Ship

To dream of a ship sailing on the sea symbolizes a project
you have taken on. If the sea is calm, the project will go
well. But if the ship is buffeted by a storm, there are likely
to be problems and difficulties ahead.

Shoes

People have been dreaming about shoes ever since
footwear was invented. It's quite a common dream theme
which reveals how you see yourself and how you think
you're getting on in life. If you dream that you're wearing
new or expensive shoes, it's an indication that you're
feeling contented and well off. The opposite to that would
be a dream about shoes that are worn out because if
someone is poor or unlucky we say they are 'down-at-heel'
or 'on their uppers' – both expressions implying that the
soles and heels are worn through and the owner can't afford
to have them mended. If you dream that you're clumping

about in great big, heavy boots or shoes, ask yourself if you've been trampling over other people's feelings lately. If your shoelaces are undone you might be about to make a mistake in your waking life. Dreaming that you have lots of pairs of shoes may be wishful thinking but it might also be suggesting that you're trying to do too much, or wanting to be in too many places at the same time. And because shoes have something to do with the steps we take in life and therefore with the progress we make, if you dream that you lose your shoes, it could mean that you're afraid of missing opportunities or chances to get ahead.
*(See also **Feet**.)*

Tom's dream

*I dreamt that I lost my **shoes**. I looked for them everywhere but I just couldn't find them. I was cross because **a band** was coming to town and I wanted to go and see them play but I couldn't until I found some shoes to wear. I don't know why I dreamt this because I've got several pairs of shoes in real life, but in that dream it was as if I only had one pair.*

Interpretation: Shoes draw our attention to feet and in our dreams feet imply walking. Walking symbolizes the progress we are making in our lives, so to lose our shoes in a dream suggests losing our way or missing out on an opportunity of some kind that limits our progress. The opportunity here is represented by a chance to go to a gig. In waking life, Tom has been learning to play the guitar and he'd been saving up for some time to buy one of his very own. He'd seen exactly the one he wanted in the music shop window in town and, what's more, it was in the sale at a knock-down price that he could just afford. The shop was shut and he decided that he would withdraw all his money from the bank and return the next day and buy the guitar then and there. Unfortunately, he couldn't get back to the shop until the next afternoon, by which time it was too late. The guitar had just been sold to someone else. It was during the following night that Tom had this dream. The band symbolizes the guitar since both are connected with music, and neither in the dream does he get to attend the gig, nor in waking life does he manage to buy the instrument. The anger he felt in the dream mirrors the anger he felt in waking life at missing such a golden opportunity to buy the guitar he wanted so badly.

Shop

Because a shop offers a variety of goods for you to pick up and buy, to dream of shopping or of being in a shop suggests the choices that you have to make in your waking life. The more indecisive you are in your dream, the more difficult you will find it to make your decisions in real life.

About sleep
It's during the periods of lighter sleep that dreaming takes place.

Silver

To see the colour silver in your dream is a good omen although, of course, gold is even better. Dreaming of a silver bracelet or chain may be warning you to check your own jewellery to make sure the clasps aren't about to break. Silver coins may mean you could be coming into a little bit of money. If you're given a silver medal in a dream, it could be your unconscious telling you to compromise in your waking life and to settle for second best.

Sister

If you had a row with your sister, or shared a secret, or went out and had a good time together, the event would have been registered in your mind and then possibly woven into a dream by your unconscious. In this case, your dream is simply mirroring that event. It may also be pointing out something about your sister, the things you like or dislike most about her. Sometimes, though, a sister in a dream may be standing in for a girlfriend or any other female, for that matter. If you've been worried about your sister, a dream that she is in danger may be bringing those anxieties to your attention.

Smell *(See Perfume.)*

Snail

Are you a bit of a dawdler, slow on the uptake or too cautious by half? Dreaming about a snail may be suggesting you are.

Snakes

A snake is said to represent sexual desire and is known in the dream business as a 'phallic symbol': it may represent a phallus or penis. Other phallic symbols include guns, knives, maypoles – in fact, anything long and thin. These sorts of dreams come under the category of erotic dreams, which means that they have a sexual meaning. You may have this sort of dream after watching a sexy movie or when you've met someone you fancy madly.
(See also Sex.)

Snow

A snowy scene may be linked to cold emotions. Have you given anyone the 'cold shoulder' recently, or have you been a bit frosty with your mates? Or perhaps this dream is warning you that someone is likely to be cold towards you in the next few days. Seeing a dazzling sheet of unblemished snow is a classic dream of purity and innocence. Dirty, trampled snow implies a feeling of guilt.

Spaceman   *(See Alien.)*

Spectacles

If you don't usually wear glasses but see yourself wearing them in your dream, it's a message telling you that you're not seeing the whole picture, that you're blinding yourself to what's going on around you in your waking life.

Spider

Because many people are terrified of spiders, to dream of them may be symbolizing something or someone they're particularly afraid of. However, according to dream lore, a spider may be a happy omen foretelling luck and good fortune.

Stage

To see yourself performing on stage either implies that you've been deceitful, 'putting on an act', or it can suggest that you have a great longing to be noticed. What role are you playing on stage? Is it the lead or do you simply have a small walk-on part? Whichever it is may describe the role you feel you have, or the role you would like to have, in your real life. If you fluff your lines, it means you lack self-confidence or that you're afraid of making a fool of yourself.

(See also Actor.)

Stairs *(See Climbing and Ladder.)*

Stars

Remember how at the infants' school the teacher would give you a star if you did a really good piece of work? Well, seeing a star in your dream means the same thing. It means you're working really hard to achieve a special goal and that if you succeed you will be rewarded for your efforts. Another way to interpret this dream is to think of it as your unconscious encouraging you to 'follow your star', that is trust yourself, be yourself and develop your own talents and abilities. Only that way will you become happy and fulfilled in your life.

Storm

Stormy weather in your dreams invariably warns of arguments and stormy emotions ahead.

Street *(See Road.)*

Sun

Just as the moon stands for the mother, women in general, or anything that's considered feminine, so the sun represents the father, men or the masculine principle. When you think of the sun you think of light, power, energy and

169

life itself. If you dream of this bright star, then, it's a way for your unconscious to tell you that you have power and imagination and inspiration inside yourself, so believe in yourself and in your ideas. It's also telling you that you have hope, so don't give up trying: look to the future because things are about to change for the better. This is an important dream which should make you feel happy for at least the rest of the day!

Sweets

Eating sweets means that you're pleased with your own efforts and you feel you deserve a reward.

Teacher

Whether there's something you need to teach someone you know or a lesson you need to learn yourself depends on whether you're the teacher or the one who is being taught in your dream. Other images will give you clues, such as what the lesson is all about, so look for information elsewhere in the dream. Take note if anything is written on the blackboard or if there are any books open on the desk as these may contain an important message.
(See also Classroom and School.)

Teeth

This is a common dream theme with several possible interpretations. On the simple physical level, this dream may be reminding you that it's high time you went to see the dentist; and you may dream of toothache if you've been grinding your teeth in your sleep – something that many people do. Symbolically, though, teeth are very much associated with our self-image and their condition in a dream is the clue to the meaning. Beautiful, white, even teeth indicate self-satisfaction, happiness and well-being. A mouthful of gnashers that are dirty or decayed suggests a disappointment, perhaps an argument with a girl/boyfriend, or a bad experience of some kind which has left you unhappy. Teeth that are loose or fall out denote loss of face or hurt pride. Or perhaps this may signify the loss of something important to you – a relationship, a good friend, a possession or some money. Visiting a dentist or having your teeth filled implies an attempt to put matters right or to face up to your problems.

Did you know that:
being too hot, too full or too uncomfortable can lead to nightmares and other vivid dreams.

Telephone

Is the amount of time you spend on the phone a bone of contention in your house? If your dad is for ever telling you to hang up or blames you for the rising cost of his phone bill, it might be that, for you, dreaming about a telephone is warning you that something irritating is about to happen. In general, though, dreaming about a telephone is quite important and you should make a note of everything that happens in this dream as soon as possible, because your unconscious is trying to give you a message here. Listen carefully to what is said over the phone as this could be vital news that you can put to good use in your waking life.

If you can't hear the speaker clearly or if the line is crackling, it could mean that you're having trouble explaining your feelings to someone in your life. Or perhaps it's telling you that you're not listening to what people are trying to say to you. A telephone that's ringing may imply that someone is about to get in touch with you.

Theatre *(See Actor.)*

Theme park

In general, theme parks and funfairs are considered places of entertainment, so this dream could be pointing to an interesting and enjoyable time ahead for you. But some of the rides provide thrills as well as spills, so if your dream takes you for a trip on a roller coaster, for example, it could well mean that events over the next few days may contain not just excitement but also some elements of fear as well. If, after your dream visit to the park, you end up elated and satisfied, that's probably how you'll soon be feeling in your waking life too.

Tiger

Tigers are beautiful and powerful creatures, so dreaming of yourself as one of these animals means you're spunky, dynamic and you've got masses of energy and willpower to get things done. If you're a tiger in your dream the message is: believe in yourself, go for it, you can do it! But if you're being chased by a tiger, it means you're afraid of something or someone in your waking life. Other images in your dream will give you clues as to who or what is frightening you. Deal with this fear by going over your dream carefully when you wake up, and imagine that you can escape or

172

throw a stone at the tiger to frighten it off. Alternatively, if you have this dream again, force yourself to turn on the tiger and shout at it until it runs away. Either way, this will help you to gain confidence and courage to deal with the problem you are facing.

*(See also **Running**.)*

Tiredness

Dreaming that you're tired can be a sign that your body needs more rest, so do yourself a favour and have a few early nights. Alternatively, this dream could be trying to tell you that you're fed up with something or someone. Perhaps you feel in a rut, tired of doing the same old thing, going to the same places, knocking around with the same old crowd. If so, think about changing your image, joining a new club, taking up a new sport or interest.

Toilet

Sitting on a toilet in a public place is the same kind of classic embarrassment dream as the one where you're walking naked down the high street with everyone staring at you. This type of dream is exposing a shy vulnerability, a fear of being 'found out'. Alternatively, of course, because going to the toilet is a means of getting rid of matter that our bodies no longer need, this sort of dream may be telling you it's time to clear out the clutter in your life. So when you wake up, give your room a good old spring clean and consider too whether there are any relationships in your life which have gone well beyond their sell-by dates. On the other hand, never forget the basics as this could simply be your unconscious nudging you to wake up because you have a full bladder and you simply have to get to the loo quick!

Train

Most moving vehicles in our dreams represent our progress in life, so to dream that you are on a train is simply reflecting the current stage that you're going through in your life. If you're enjoying the journey, life's OK, but if you're afraid or unhappy, your dream is telling you there are things (or people) in your waking life that are troubling you. If the train stops and refuses to budge any further, it could mean that you're not making the sort of progress in your life that you would like. Perhaps a relationship isn't going the way you want or perhaps you're not doing as well as you would like in your school work. If you miss a train, your dream may be warning you not to miss a good opportunity.

Treasure

To be given some treasure may be predicting that you'll come into money quite soon. To come across a pile of treasure may mean that you will discover something special about yourself. Perhaps you'll suddenly find you have a particular talent or gift you didn't know about or hadn't recognised about yourself in the past. Or it's possible that this dream is telling you that your ideas are original and you should value them instead of thinking they're worthless.

Tree *(See Forest.)*

Tunnel

Tunnels make fascinating, and sometimes frightening, dream symbols. To dream that you're lost in a dark tunnel and can't find your way out can be a really frightening nightmare. This dream may be telling you that you're somehow feeling trapped in real life or that you want to escape from your responsibilities. Or it may be saying that you're finding a problem difficult to solve, or that you simply can't find what (or who) you're looking for. To dream of a car or a train hurtling through a tunnel and rushing towards you may be warning you of trouble ahead. Perhaps you're on a 'collision course' with a friend and about to have an almighty row. If you dream about walking through a dark tunnel but see a pinprick of light at the end, your unconscious is telling you that you're coming to the end of your problems or that a period of unhappiness will soon be over. The nearer you are to the end of the tunnel, the sooner you'll find happiness again. If you dream of walking through a tunnel and straight out the other end into the sunshine, it's a sign of new developments, perhaps a new adventure or a new phase in your life that is about to start.

(See also Sex.)

Did you know that:
drugs and alcohol interfere with our ability to dream and our brains may be forced to hallucinate in the daytime instead in order to make up for this lack of dreaming time.

Umbrella

To dream that you're under an umbrella is a sign that you are being sheltered and protected from the problems in life.

Uniform

Apart from school kids, uniforms are associated with people in authority. So, a dream about uniforms usually has something to do with rules and regulations in general or with a particular authority figure.

University

Because it is a place of learning, to dream of a university is like dreaming of teachers and schools, which means that you feel you either have to teach someone a lesson or you have something important to learn.
(See also Classroom.)

Vampire

Because vampires are blood-sucking creatures, a dream of one may be telling you that someone you know, or some activity that you're involved in, is a drain on your energy.

Vegetables

Although lovely, fresh, crisp vegetables are a sign of life and vitality, certain individual vegetables like cabbages and potatoes may be suggesting that your life is a bit dull at present, or that you're 'vegetating' away. Are you a couch potato, perhaps, or a bit of a limp lettuce? If that's the case, you need to try a new image or to find a way of putting the sparkle back into your waking life. Otherwise, the meaning of the dream may not so much be found in the

176

actual vegetable itself, but in its colour, so that a bunch of cress, for example, is a symbolic green or a radish stands for the colour red. (See under **Colour** for the meanings of these.)

Volcano

If you've been feeling angry and frustrated lately, you may well dream about a volcano. Alternatively, this dream may be warning you that someone you know is about to blow his/her top. Whichever it is, emotions are on the boil.

Voyage *(See Journey and Walking.)*

W

Walking

This dream has the same sort of meaning as all the other dreams about travel and transport, except that here you're walking and not riding a bike, car, train or horse. Essentially, they're the same because in all of them there's the sense of moving forwards and this symbolizes your progress through life. If you're strolling along and enjoying the scenery, your unconscious is telling you that you're finding life quite OK at present; in fact, you're altogether contented. If you're dawdling along in your dream and then find you've missed your bus, it may be telling you not to be so laid back in your waking life because you're missing opportunities or because you're not developing your talents. So this dream is saying: get a move on! If your walk is taking you up a steep hill, you may be having some difficulties in your life: perhaps you're finding it hard to keep up in class, or you're struggling with a subject you don't like. If it's a big mountain you're trying to walk up, you may be feeling overwhelmed by problems, or by your relationships. Obstacles in your way, either a boulder, a deep pit, or a broken bridge all represent challenges that you may encounter. Being confused about how to get around the obstacles warns of complications. Getting over the obstacles, though, means that you will succeed in getting over your difficulties in life. The scenery is very important in this type of dream because it symbolizes what is going on around you in real life. If the scenery is pleasant, for example, life is pleasant. But if the background is horrid, dirty, barren or broken down, it's suggesting that you're finding things tough or unpleasant right now.

About sleep

You can tell when people are dreaming because you can see their eyeballs rolling around beneath their closed eyelids just as if they were watching a movie on a big screen. Scientists call this phenomenon REM, or rapid eye movement, so that the period when we dream is known as REM sleep. The deeper sleep, when we don't dream, is called NREM sleep, or non-rapid eye movement sleep.

Wall

Do you feel you're being blocked or stonewalled or hemmed in in some way? Dreaming of a wall may be suggesting you are. If there's any way you can see beyond the wall or go around it, you'll be able to see a way out of the problem you're facing in your waking life.

War

To dream that you are caught in the middle of a war suggests that life for you is difficult or full of conflict at the moment.

Washing

If you're having a wash it means you want to make a fresh start. Perhaps you're washing away a feeling of guilt or a bad experience, or perhaps you're 'washing your hands' of the whole affair, which means you no longer want to take part in something that's going on in your waking life at the moment. The same message applies if you're washing clothes. It means you want to put the past behind you and start over again.
(*See also* **Bath** *and* **Water**.)

Wasp

Either you're annoying someone or someone is annoying you. Alternatively, you may have been 'stung' by a friend's hurtful comments about you.

Watch

Time is ticking by.
(*See also* **Clock**.)

Water

Dreams about water symbolize our emotions. Gazing out at a calm lake says that you are emotionally well-balanced and that you have your feelings well under control. A

torrential rain storm, a raging river or a wild sea all
suggest that your emotions are turbulent and possibly in
for a bit of a battering, like when you fall out with a
friend, when a teacher tells you off or when you have a
row with your mum and dad. If you're drowning in water,
it means you're finding it difficult to cope with your
responsibilities. Dirty, murky water means that you can't
see a problem clearly, so it's warning you of confusion or
complications. If the water is stagnant, your unconscious
is hinting that your life is at a bit of a standstill. Perhaps
it's time for you to develop some new interests or make
new friends.
*(See also **Boats**.)*

Hannah's dream

*While **swimming in a pool**, I felt myself being dragged
under the water. I fought to come up again but as I
reached the surface, **a girl pushed me back** under. All
I could see was the surface getting further and further
away. I woke up with a jump.*

Interpretation: Water in our dreams symbolizes our
emotions. The fact that Hannah is being dragged under
suggests that in her waking life she is being overwhelmed
by her feelings. Reaching the surface tells her that she
sometimes manages to get on top of her emotions. However, just as she nearly succeeds in controlling her
feelings, she is pushed under again which means that all
those feelings come flooding back and overpower her
once more. Seeing the surface receding means that she
thinks she will never be able to get on top of the situation.
What is important in this dream is to find out whether
Hannah recognizes the girl who is pushing her under. And
in fact she does – only too well. It transpires that the girl

in Hannah's dream is a rival of hers because she is the person who stole Hannah's boyfriend away from her. Now, every time Hannah sees that girl in waking life, she experiences overwhelming anger and sadness and jealousy, but there's little she can do because the boyfriend has made it plain he no longer wants to see Hannah as he's now in love with the other girl. What might help Hannah in this situation is for her to sit quietly and go over this dream in her own mind several times but each time try to continue the dream and make up a really satisfying ending. Perhaps she could think of swimming away underwater and breaking the surface right into the arms of the most gorgeous hunk she's ever laid eyes on and, as they fall in love, she realizes how little her previous boyfriend means to her now. Adding our own endings to a dream or a nightmare is quite a good trick to help us get over unhappy experiences because it gives us hope and encouragement that things will get better in the future. It's called positive thinking, and if you think positively, you start to feel better and you attract positive situations to you. Try it: it works!

Waterfall

This is a beautiful symbol of hope for the future since the splashing water washes away all the old problems and prepares you for a new beginning. The message is: don't look back.

Wedding *(See Bride and bridegroom.)*

Well *(See Water.)*

Wig

A wig is worn to change one's appearance, so a dream in which you're wearing a wig is suggesting that you're behaving out of character in your waking life. Are you experimenting with a new image or do you feel you have to change to fit in with a different group? Are you putting on airs, perhaps, pretending you're someone you're not? If the wig fits perfectly and looks good on you, then your change of image is successful. If the wig keeps slipping off or doesn't suit you at all, your unconscious is telling you that you're not really comfortable in your new role and that you'd be a lot happier just being yourself.

Did you know that:
animals also dream – you can always tell when your dog is dreaming that he's chasing next door's cat because his legs start to twitch!

Window

Take note of what you can see through your dream window as this will give you an insight into future events. If the scene is pleasant, like a garden for example, it means that life is smooth and contented at present. If all you can see through the window is rocks or rubble, this is a warning of trouble ahead. A mountain suggests hard work; a volcano warns of explosive feelings; a brick wall suggests frustration. A sunny scene predicts happiness, a still lake promises peace of mind, and a pile of treasure means that you may soon be coming into some money.

Wolf

Think of all the stories and sayings you know about wolves. They are frequently about deceit and deception: for example, wolves in sheep's clothing and the tale of *Little Red Riding Hood*. So if you dream about a wolf, it's a warning to be careful whom you trust because someone is out to put one over on you.

Woods *(See Forest.)*

Zoo

If you dream that you're having a pleasant day out at the zoo, it suggests that you'll be meeting new people and having a good time soon. If the animals looked unhappy in their cages, your dream may be telling you that you feel trapped either by a problem or by the situation you're in, in your waking life. If the animals escape, it may be your unconscious telling you that you too can find a way out of your problems.

Notes

_____
_____
_____
_____
_____
_____
_____
_____
_____
_____
_____
_____
_____
_____
_____
_____
_____
_____
_____
_____

Notes

Notes

Notes

Notes